A Young Lady's Miscellany

Also by Auriel Roe

A Blindefellows Chronicle

Let The Swine Go Forth

A Young Lady's Miscellany

Auriel Roe

Dogberry Books

Cover design by Andriy Dankovych
www.davart.com.ua

For Manda & May

A *Young Lady's Miscellany* by Auriel Roe

Contents

1

On Grandmothers & Girlhood

Warm and cold, fat and thin, open and closed...I saw my grandmothers as opposites. Amanda 'Manda' Mossop, my paternal grandmother, born 1907, Edwardian and named after both her mother and grandmother. May, just May, Fielding, my maternal grandmother, born 1896, Victorian and named after Princess May of Teck, a royal of the time.

Their differences could be spotted even in their handwriting in birthday cards. When May wrote 'Nana' in her spikey italic, it looked more like 'haha', which was a family joke as she was not known for her sense of humour. Manda didn't have May's controlled penmanship. Her writing was luxuriantly loopy with rough kisses at the end, rather like the signatures of her illiterate grandparents.

As the times and their class dictated, both left school at fourteen. Manda went straight into 'service' as a maid, while May, who had an artistic side, dreamt of becoming a milliner. This was scoffed at due to her weak eyesight so instead she went to work at the Co-op in Rochdale, where her creative hands folded sheets of paper into neat little bags to fill with oatmeal.

Again, as the times dictated, both gave up their jobs when they married, Manda to Wilfred or 'Wiff', and May to Joseph. Wiff was a small, wiry fellow who looked like Fred Astaire. Manda was no Ginger Rogers though and often compared herself to another actor, Fatty Arbuckle. I have inherited her sturdy calves. Despite his slight frame, Wiff cycled eight miles each way in all weathers across arduous terrain to his job at the steel works in Workington and, when I was little, enjoyed drawing detailed diagrams of the smelting furnace for me.

May met Joseph at a tea dance for soldiers convalescing from the traumas of World War I. When he felt recovered, they married and he returned to the job he did before the war, under-manager of a coal mine. They had four children and May became a widow in her fifties with free coal for the rest of her life.

Whitehaven, the West Cumbrian town where my parents grew up, is moulded like a spoon, with the town centre and harbour at the base of the bowl and the bulk of the residential housing on the slopes around. On visits there, I had a sense of drawing the short straw regarding where I slept because, being the youngest, I would spend the night at May's with my mother. May lived in a drafty, semi-detached house on the fittingly named Hilltop Road, with the smell of the Irish Sea in the back garden. It was one of the highest and therefore most wind-battered roads in Whitehaven. My two sisters, on the other hand, stayed in the guest room of Manda's two up, two down terraced house on Main Street in the suburb of Hensingham on the other side of town.

Fortunately for them, Manda lived opposite Bob's Fish and Chips and Mary Jordan's Sweet Shop. They had cuddles against Manda's ample bosom, whereas I had none against May's rail thin torso.

The houses of my grandmothers both had popular pebble-dashed exteriors, the purveyors of which claimed it was an extra layer against the northern chill, albeit a flimsy one. Each house also had a parlour, a room that was barely used, set aside for milestone feasts from cradle to grave: christenings, Christmases, birthdays, weddings, funerals. Both of these parlours had eventually become obsolete, their fireplaces sealed off. Wakes for funerals, for instance, were now held in the local pub where soup and sandwiches were served—very necessary after the bitter cold of a Cumbrian graveyard.

When you walked through Manda's never locked front door, you were in her parlour. No one stopped to sit on the suite upholstered in red poppies on a cream background. Neither did they pay attention to the vase decorated with two canoodling budgerigars, nor the engraved steel tray my grandfather had been presented with on his retirement, both of which were placed on a stout curved sideboard that reminded me of an early wireless. When people dropped in on Manda, which they did a lot, they didn't loiter in this chilly parlour but strode right through into her snug little sitting room at the back for a cup of tea, and probably some of her homemade shortbread, along with a retelling of the latest scandals, which she gobbled up with cries of 'She never did!' and 'He said what?' She was ever the astonished listener, rarely the teller of tales.

May's parlour was behind a closed door off the hallway, rather than being a thoroughfare. It was untouched by human breath and as frigid as the tomb. Nevertheless, boredom often led me into that room while my mother helped her mother with this and that. The furniture in this parlour was bought early in her marriage during the 1920s, but was not the stylish Art Deco variety, just plain, solid and practical. The smart dining room table was left permanently folded against the wall through lack of use. There were two stacks of dining room chairs to serve as a reminder of the once large family gatherings that had taken place there decades earlier. A couple of the wing-backed armchairs May favoured faced the empty hearth. The glass doors of the bookcase were rarely opened. On the shelf inside it was a long row of mining handbooks with gold embossed writing on the spines. Occasionally, I took one out to leaf through. They were filled with blueprint-like diagrams, very different from the sketches drawn for me by Grandad Wiff.

Tucked in at the end of these mining books was, I supposed, May's only book apart from those containing recipes. It was called *A Young Lady's Miscellany* and was chock-full of cautionary tales concerning young ladies facing dire situations who triumphed when they kept their moral wits about them, such as in 'The Artful Seducer or A Warning to Young Women'.

Who the writers were was unclear as most of it was anonymous. 'By a Clergyman' often appeared at the end, or sometimes 'By a Mournful Husband', or 'A father's advice to his daughter'. Poetry was interspersed, again laden with moral messages and with peculiar titles such as 'On A Lady's Muff', a scathing attack on vanity. Stories of family strife appeared too, such as 'A Tale of an Indolent Sibling', which was about a brother who wouldn't get up for work in the morning so the mother and the sister prepared a tantalising breakfast, and when that didn't work, battered him out of bed with carpet beaters. Amongst these stories were illustrated pages that proffered practical tips about how to bleach bloomers or darn a stocking. It was a well-thumbed tome and I imagine May was very familiar with everything in it.

With my interest in animals, I liked to rearrange the china birds that were placed across the mantle-piece in May's parlour. On one occasion, however, a greenfinch fell from my hand and broke into pieces on the tiles below. I was too afraid to tell May. I knew she could be strict about trivial matters. She had once reprimanded me when I fed the birds in the garden with what was, unbeknownst to me, the sacred crusts at either end of a loaf of sliced white bread...'You cannot throw the crusts to the birds. They keep the bread fresh!' she'd scolded, wagging a bony index finger, unaware that Britain had entered the age of preservatives. I was determined not to be subjected to the wagging finger again so I tip-toed into the sitting room where my mother was finding her mother a specific button, in a tin full of hundreds of buttons, to match the dress she was finishing off sewing. Nonchalantly, I took the glue from the kitchen drawer and returned to the parlour, repairing the fractured ornament as well as a reasonably dextrous child of eight could. I then attempted to obscure it slightly behind the carriage clock in the middle of the mantelpiece as the glue was making an unsightly yellow seam.

The next day, May asked me why I hadn't told her I'd broken the bird. She wasn't cross; there was no wagging finger. She must have spotted me with the glue and gone to investigate. Perhaps she realised that I couldn't bring myself to tell her about the mishap and it is possible she even felt sorry for me. After that, I became a little less scared of her.

I was well aware that my sisters would be raiding the cupboard under the stairs for sugary titbits stored in old biscuit tins at Manda's but at May's there was a superior class of baked goods which often involved dried fruit and with peculiar names from another age: Dates Cut and Come Again, Sly Cake, York Plum Slice. In the past, May had wrapped these energy rich rations in waxed paper for her husband down the mine. These and other marvels were created in my favourite place in the house, the pantry, a little L-shaped room off the kitchen with a cold marble countertop perfect for rolling out pastry. There was really only enough space for one in there, although on occasion, May permitted a grandchild to help put the ginger sponge cubes onto a plate or mix a Yorkshire pudding batter. Ginger sponge, a rich dark cake baked in a deep square tin, always came out with a chewy, treacly top. It was cut into perfect cubes and, despite being the moistest of cakes, spreading butter on one side of it was the rule.

The shelves lining the pantry walls were crammed with canisters labelled in May's sloping Victorian

hand: dark chocolate drops, flaked almonds, or cand-
ied peel May made herself, having been brought up
in the mill town of Rochdale with the mantra of
'Waste not, Want not' in the days when the peel of a
rare orange was precious. Being a hungry child with
a sweet tooth, I'd frequently have a bit of a graze in
these canisters when no one was looking, and would
sometimes overdo it to the point of nausea.

May was also an expert in cooked dinners, although her early twentieth century cuisine could be
on the grisly side. Sometimes, a terrible stench
would envelop the kitchen and, on lifting the lid of a
saucepan, it was possible to see an entire sheep's
head bubbling within, its eyes fixing you in a steamy
glare. Pigs' heads were also boiled, snout facing the
ceiling, as if they were trophies mounted in the pot
as they would have been upon the wall.

When May had married at the age of twenty-
three, she had stepped into the role of housewife
with gusto, as if all her life had been leading up to
that moment. From a young age, she and her sisters
had been sewing and embroidering items that each
of them added to their own 'bottom drawer'
trousseau. When May's oldest sister married and
went off to live in Australia, much indignation was
caused by the photograph she sent home. In this
picture, which showed her with her husband in their
new dining room, May spotted one of the tablecloths
she had made and let fly with her life-long expletive
of 'Oh, my Godfather!'. The sister had helped herself
to it from May's bottom drawer so May never spoke
to her again.

Apart from the parlour and the pantry, there were

a few other amusements at May's, such as finding colonies of woodlice under loose bricks in the garden. I would gather these in a zinc bucket and, when I had a goodly number, put my arm in and enjoy the sensation of having their multitudes crawl over me. A strange desire but stranger still was one of my older sister's habits when, as a toddler, she would collect worms in a blue melamine cup and then eat them, claiming they tasted like spam, one of our staples. This particular sister was notoriously hungry and, as a baby, would begin to weep piteously whenever the spoon started to scrape the bottom of the dish.

Another diversion at May's was the collapsing wooden shack at the back which was inhabited by wild cats. For obvious reasons, I wasn't allowed inside it to befriend the creatures but I would sneak out saucers of milk and wait at the window. One of them would eventually dart out, low to the ground, and invariably upset the saucer.

May was the most ancient person I'd ever known, even older than my first teacher, the draconian Miss Read. My mother was the last of her four children and she was already in her seventies when I was born. She was always decked out in garb that was otherwise extinct: nylons and sensible shoes with a low heel, plain but sometimes with some subtle adornment like a buckle or a bow and handmade knee-length dresses of the type worn in the 1930s, with a slightly ornamental bodice, often featuring pearly buttons. The dresses were dark brown or bottle green, never 'showy', but immaculately stitched as she was an expert seamstress, despite the poor eyesight that had forced her into her career involving oatmeal.

When she took the bus to bingo in the town centre, as she did once a week right into her nineties, she wore a fur hat and a musquash coat. This may seem a little grand for the simplicity of legs eleven and two little ducks but the prize money was considerable and she dressed in readiness for the occasion when she would go onstage to receive her rich winnings before the congregation of envious elders. As almost all old ladies in Britain did up until the 1990s, she kept her grey hair short, curling it herself, but most certainly did not sport one of those 'common' coloured rinses. She paid close attention to people's appearances, 'What's her name? The tidy body around the corner', would be how she identified someone of whose appearance she approved. May certainly didn't approve of Manda's fashion choices, however, which were somewhat stuck in the 1960s: form-fitting polyester pinafores with swirling brightly-coloured psychedelic patterns, all damped down with a dull rain mac and a clear plastic head scarf when she went out. Yet, in spite of their sartorial differences, both concurred in never sinking to the unfeminine depth of donning trousers, even in pyjama form.

In the sitting room, May's personal armchair was positioned nearest to the coal fire. On one occasion, trying to get myself warm, I sat in this chair while she was working in the kitchen. She was astonished to see me there and exclaimed 'Oh, my Godfather! Would you jump into my grave as fast?', which made me change my seat with extreme celerity.

Owing to her poor eyesight, her armchair was also nearest to the television. She watched it for several hours a day, often becoming furious at the content of those programmes that revealed the dreadful decline in modern day morals. One of her favourite phrases was, 'They should be put up against a brick wall and shot'. This fate was meted out once to The New Seekers, singers of such subversive hits as 'I'd Like to Teach the World to Sing', due to the girls' having 'long loose hair'. She held strong views of an extreme type for reasons I could not fathom. She described the teenage Lady Diana when she was first being reluctantly strewn across the media as having 'a sly look about her'.

I dreaded bedtime at May's and would put off going upstairs as long as possible because it was freezing up there and I didn't want to leave the fire in the sitting room. I would, therefore, stay up until nearly midnight watching snooker with my mother and May on the black and white television, which was quite a feat when trying to follow the game. Show jumping was another of May's favourites. Indeed, one of my earliest memories entails the time the show-jumper, Harvey Smith, flicked a V at the judges. In response to this, May shouted out in astonishment, 'Oh, my Godfather! Did you see what he just did? Why, he did that!' whereupon she flicked a wide V at my mother, who was so mortified that she tried to put her hand over my eyes. It must have had a profound effect upon me to see this late Victorian, prim and proper lady contorted into a gesture of profanity because it has remained vivid in my memory.

Eventually, I would reach the point when I could stay awake no longer in the stiff-backed armchairs. I would brush my teeth in the bathroom just off the kitchen, heated by a spluttering and pungent paraffin stove, brace myself and trudge upstairs into the Arctic Circle above. There were three rooms, May's, my mother's old room, now 'the sewing room' and Jim's room. Jim was a strange old uncle who had never left home and refrained from socialising. My allocated place of repose was in the corner of May's room in a nylon sleeping bag on a camp-bed that consisted of a piece of canvas hooked onto a wobbly frame with rusting springs. I had to sleep there with caution as a sudden move could result in the bed jackknifing, trapping me inside it. I didn't like sleeping on the camp-bed but it was preferable to where my mother slept, in the double bed *with* May. Part of me blanched at the idea of being so physically close to May and I was convinced she'd have sharp, snaggled toe nails under the sheets.

May's bedroom was crowded with dark-stained early twentieth century wooden furnishings. In the corner was a solid and plain dressing table on which was propped a sepia photograph of my grandfather, Joseph, who had died suddenly at home of an aneurysm, leaving May a widow at fifty-six. My fourteen-year-old mother was sent out in haste to buy bicarbonate of soda as a cure for his pain. When she returned, he was dead.

Joseph's eyes regarded me as soon as I entered the room each night but I knew he had been a good person so I wasn't afraid. As a young man, he'd fought right through the first world war on horse

-back and, miraculously, both he and his horse, Billy had survived. While he was in France, he'd received the news that his first wife, Florence Tickle, had died as a result of her diabetes. Their toddler son was thereafter brought up by Florence's parents. After the war, though uninjured, Joseph was placed in a convalescent home for soldiers, which hinted at a mental trauma he never spoke about in front of his children. As an under-manager of Haig Pit, he was known for his care for others. He'd once dragged his boss out of a tunnel by his boots when he'd collapsed in front of him, saving him from the deadly blackdamp. When her grandchildren arrived, May made each of them an intricately crafted stuffed toy using fabric from Joseph's clothes. Perhaps this was because they had hung in the wardrobe untouched for years, but also, perhaps, to give each of us a little piece of the grandfather we'd never known.

The sewing room could have been a plausible place to put up a grandchild but there was a heavy wrought iron Singer sewing machine table in the middle of it, along with bolts of cloth and old suitcases, which left no room for a camp-bed. This came as a relief since, when it was my mother's room as a girl, she had often wondered why the crack of dark where the attic hatch met the ceiling sometimes rose slightly and then fell again, as if the old house were breathing. Once or twice, she'd had a dream that a pair of eyes was looking down at her from there.

Inside my sleeping bag, I wore flannel pyjamas, along with a pair of knitted bedsocks with the drawstrings done up at the ankles. Anyone who dared to stay the night at May's was presented with bedsocks. She could churn out a pair on her knitting needles in a few hours, always in a hotch-potch of colours as they were made of odds and ends of wool. I liked them so much, I'd take the pair back home to Yorkshire and wear them round the house until they got holes and my toes poked through.

My feet were reasonably warm but my nose was a chip of ice and the sleeping bag was woefully under-stuffed for the tundra of Hilltop Road. With the sleeping bag cinched around my head and just my mottled nose sticking out, I probably resembled a pig's head in a saucepan. Whenever I tentatively changed position, the springs creaked and I was never entirely warm. Eventually, I would drift off and the next thing I would be aware of was watery light coming through the curtains and the smell of toast and rum butter wafting up the staircase.

Rum butter was a staple of the Cumbrian miners' diet and, even with all the coal mines closed, its popularity barely waned. Many Cumbrians, despite their sedentary modern lives, continue to consume this calorific concoction partly out of a regional pride that has often helped lead them to the ultimate sedentary experience of an early grave from arteriosclerosis. It probably didn't help that one of the traditions following christenings was to put rum butter on the baby's dummy at the gathering in the parlour, so that it was the first thing Cumbrians ever ate, myself included. May, however, downed lashings of the stuff yet didn't put on an ounce and lived a long life.

One particular morning, my mother had prepared the toast but the moment May took a bite, she made a face of ghoulish disdain, 'What's this?' she said, her mouth full of the stuff, 'There's no butter *under* the rum butter!' My mother tried to reason with her, saying that butter would be surplus as rum butter was, well, mainly butter but May would have none of it.

There are many Cumbrian legends surrounding the mysterious origins of rum butter. My favourite is the tale of the smugglers forced to hide with their booty in a cave on the coast of St Bees. The customs and excise men patrolling the cliffs above expected the bodies to float out with the incoming tide but they didn't realise there was a chamber in the cave that remained above sea level so the smugglers were able to wait it out. No doubt these details were intended to lend some credibility to the tale. In time, the smugglers became peckish. Conveniently, one of them happened to have a pat of butter on him, as one does when out smuggling. They came up with the cunning plan of mixing this into a paste with their smuggled rum and sugar, which turned out to be so pleasing that a new regional confection was born.

Like most people in Whitehaven, May made her own rum butter, poured it into cut glass sugar basins, patted it down and left it to set in the pantry. Hers was dark due to the extra rum she put in. She ate it every day and burned off the calories making the coal fire, swabbing her grate, taking an axe out back to chop kindling, and wringing out clothes until they were virtually dry with her sinewy blue-veined hands. All of these chores were carried out in her smart 1930s dress, nylon tights and court shoes.

In her late eighties, May had her first brush with death. She'd been down in the town centre attending her weekly bingo bonanza in her musquash coat and, as was her custom, returned on the late bus at around 11 pm. It dropped her off at the end of Hilltop Road but walking the rest of the way home, she had fallen into a hole left unmarked by the gas company. When she came to, there was a man looking down at her, sizing her up. 'Is that you, May?' he asked. With a shudder, she realised it was Mr. Mirth, the undertaker who was out walking his whippet. She was a little the worse for wear after this mishap and had a spell in the geriatric ward at the West Cumberland Hospital. Despite being one of the older patients, she was still very much in command of her marbles and called for the nurse whenever something outlandish occurred, such as when the lady in the bed next to her began buttering her napkin instead of her toast.

When I was nine, my oldest sister left home and thenceforth rarely accompanied us to Whitehaven. My other sister was thereafter put up with a cousin of her age and I was billetted at Manda's. I don't know why the change occured; perhaps I'd grown out of the camp-bed, or maybe it had finally been acknowledged that this was an awfully uncomfortable way to pass the night, especially now the massive double bed in Manda's guest room was available.

Like the parlour below it, Manda and Wiff's guest room saw little use. They were squashed in a low-to-the-ground, sagging double bed in the back bedroom with barely enough room to shuffle around the bed if the toilet beckoned in the night. There was, however, a small square window which looked out onto the tranquil meadow at the back. Perhaps they were partial to the view and the quiet away from the street, which could be noisy. I like to think this but probably it was because they saved the larger room with the best bed for visitors. As there was no room for furniture in their tiny room, they kept their clothes in the front bedroom in the same typically dour, dark, heavy wooden furniture that May and most working class British old people had at the time.

Staying at Manda's intensified my penchant for fish and chips. I was something of a sickly child, allergic to most foods, but fish and chips was a rare treat I could eat without unfortunate consequences. Directly opposite Manda's house was Bob's Fish and Chips, which I would patronize almost nightly when I stayed there, relishing my meal with a bottle of pop, usually Dandelion and Burdock. Bob was a cheerful, diminutive man with a smart moustache and a withered arm, a war wound of the fish and chip industry. Bob's chip shop had been there for years and when, at an advanced age, he finally retired to focus on canary breeding, fish and chips continued to be sold from the premises but they were never as good. The new owners didn't scatter your chips with the batter 'scraps', for example, which was a particular delight for a child who was perpetually peckish. When Bob died in his nineties, his funeral cortege paused at his old chippy for a final farewell and the new fryers stood outside and doffed their white hats.

I ate my fish and chips in the evening on the fold-out tray table in front of the fire, which was now gas as making a coal fire had become too burdensome for Manda and Wiff. This was a great shame for me as making a coal fire was one of my few talents. Sometimes Wiff would go out for a pint and return with a bag of crisps for me containing a twist of salt and a pickled onion for the vinegar. As the night wore on, there'd be cards, also on the tray table, which was absorbing as no one had ever taught me these old-time pursuits before. Grandad Wiff would sketch a labelled diagram of a furnace for me and, like a human furnace, would delight me with blowing cigarette smoke out of his nose. He couldn't quite manage it when I asked him to blow smoke out of his ears too. I would then pluck his glasses off his face and polish away all the smudges that he said he hadn't noticed in the slightest before his lenses were cleaned.

There was a lot to look forward to in the daytime, too. The meadow at the back of the house was an overgrown wilderness. Manda and I would go out there to pick blackcurrants, taking care that she didn't get a ladder in her support tights. Then we'd make an apple and blackcurrant pie, which she'd remove from the oven with a threadbare dishcloth. Her hands were worn smooth and shiny in places, seemingly heatproof. The slices of pie were served drenched in a pool of evaporated milk.

At the end of the meadow was a path that ran alongside an old sandstone wall. Taking the left fork, you came to the post office where Manda would collect the pensions. This was next to an old

Weslyan chapel that looked like a miniature castle, which had prompted my sisters to call it The Witch's House which, in turn prompted me to give it a wide berth. Beyond this was a small library which seemed to cater exclusively to the elderly. Here Manda would borrow bodice rippers by the bag full, with titles like *Ride the Storm* and *A Savage Adoration*, her reading choices hinting at earthy inclinations. Taking the right fork, you came to Cartgate Mansion, owned by the ironically named Mrs. Halfpenny. Wiff occasionally cleaned windows there and it was a lucky day indeed when he took me along with him. Mrs. Halfpenny, via Wiff, gave me permission to pick a bunch of the purple crocuses dotted about in the lush parkland at the front. I'd caught occasional glimpses of the widowed Mrs. Halfpenny, smiling in her tennis whites as she play-ed matches on her private court.

After the window cleaning, Wiff and I would continue on to his tidy allotment, where he'd gather what was needed for the next few days in Manda's kitchen. We'd sit on the bench alongside his little shed, eating what he regarded as the best kind of apple, one that was slightly aged with a crinkly skin. Along with the shallots stored in a chicken wire hammock slung from the ceiling, he had a few waif-like pin-ups in the shed, including one of Audrey Hepburn. I used to think how they all looked so unlike Manda, who had been strong and solid since her youth.

When midnight approached, with Manda's being a smaller, warmer house than May's, I did not dread going up to bed. After a few games of cards, I'd climb the narrow staircase, just in time to watch the drunks being disgorged from the pub opposite, engaged in staggering, weaving antics that were fascinating to a child. Eventually, they'd all slope off and I'd sink into a deep and undisturbed sleep under a warm, pink eiderdown, to be woken the next morning by Manda's cheerful, dewlapped face popping into the room to say, 'Hello beautiful dreamer, come down and have some nice warm toast and rum butter with your nana and grandad'. I didn't know it yet but soon there would come a time when her kindness would keep me from sinking entirely into the abyss.

2

Acquiring Awareness of the World & its Ways

My father was an ambitious man who couldn't resist pursuing jobs of a higher status. As is the way, the accompanying spouse and dependents were moved hither and thither as he realised those ambitions. All too soon, he'd get itchy feet and we'd be off again to another house, another school. When I was around eight, he was offered a job with an extraordinary salary to manage the construction of a sewage system in Saudi Arabia. Such was the exotic nature of news like that back then that *The Selby Times* dispatched a reporter and a photographer to our house and ran a feature with us on the front page, arranged on the couch in our sitting room. After going to Saudi for a few weeks to try it out, he decided against this career move when he learnt he'd be held responsible, possibly losing his life, or at least his hands, should the construction go awry.

My father had managed to get into Whitehaven's grammar school as a boy, probably helped by his sporting prowess, extreme confidence and a twinkling green eye. After fooling around throughout, he left school at sixteen with almost no qualifications. Normally, this would have meant a job down the mine, which was exactly what happened but, due to some kindly last minute intervention, he went not as a miner but as a trainee surveyor. He didn't like it though. Being underground made him nervous. When he was a child he had watched them bring out the bodies following the William Pit disaster, in which over a hundred miners were killed. Fortunately for him, the mines were starting to close and he was soon offered alternative training in productivity management. This led to his next two jobs in now extinct factories: British Rope in Sunderland, followed by The Plastic Factory in Egremont, having returned to Cumbria because he missed his mates. Here my older sisters were offered up as reluctant models for a range of vinyl children's handbags. These were his first few rungs on the management ladder. He never made it to the pinnacle because he fell off while under the influence in his fifties.

About midway through his ascent, we moved, one summer, to Caerleon in South Wales, where he had been given a job as the production manager of a cable factory. There was the usual traipsing around houses for sale and, as was always the case, I was more attracted to the older properties with the higgledy-piggledy warrens of rooms and the slightly overgrown gardens. In one such place that looked out onto a village green, I strayed from my parents and came across a middle-aged man changing a baby whilst smoking a pipe. I briefly marvelled at his ability to do this, then imagined him misplacing the pipe and smoke emerging from the baby's nappy.

My parents' taste in houses was different to mine.

They preferred the plain modern box to the idio-syncratic historical edifice. In the midst of house viewings on one occasion, they had paid for a tour of a nearby stately home and afterwards I had asked if they could buy that one, please.

I wasn't too displeased with the house they bought in Caerleon which, although it was just a plain red brick rectangular cube, did have a large garden with secret pathways through rhododendron bushes. It was at the end of a cul-de-sac and, as the urban sprawl had paused at our house, countryside walks were temporarily on the doorstep. This meant that my wish to have a dog was finally granted.

Getting a dog was a big step for my parents as neither of them had grown up with one. As a girl, my mother had been given a white rabbit with pink eyes, but the dog from next door managed to get into the hutch and made off with it. She had last seen it dangling from the miscreant hound's jowls. This had put her off entertaining the idea of having a dog herself but, after a couple of hamsters and a terra-pin, I had proven myself responsible enough to receive the ultimate pet. The hamsters succumbed to natural causes at the ripe old age of two, but the fate of the terrapin puzzles me to this day. Hardly a gregarious pet, it lived out its life upon a stone in a fishbowl, endlessly staring at some fixed point on the ceiling. One day, on closer inspection, I noticed that the living terrapin had been replaced by a ceramic one. I relayed this observation to the family and they were equally baffled. No one ever owned up to the switch so, for some time, I believed the unfortunate reptile had been petrified by a dark force.

My mother decided it was the right thing to do to adopt an abandoned dog. In the animal shelters at that time, they put dogs down if they weren't adopted within a few weeks. Dog shelters in those days stank to high heaven. You could smell canine urine on the air within a half mile radius, unless you were a dog, in which case it was a fifteen mile radius.

I was ten when, with my sister, I entered the death row enclosure to choose just one of the doomed animals. My sister's face was soggy with tears and I felt the same way but was, as usual, suppressing it. I liked a friendly little knock-kneed sausage dog with outward-turned feet, but my sister convinced my mother to adopt a golden retriever, larger than what they'd planned for but in a pitiful state. The dog sat, dejected, at the back of her enclosure, rake thin, ears down. She showed signs of giving birth recently but the dog catcher had seen no puppies on the waste ground where she was found. After a few baths to get rid of the smell of the shelter, Jess soon settled in with us. She was quick to learn the usual sit, give the paw, lie down and jump through a hoop, but she was hopeless at catching, hence her nickname, Buttermouth.

I was slightly dreading the end of the summer holidays as I was due to start at the comprehensive school on the ominously named Cold Bath Road. There was a rumour that this is what the new pupils received as an initiation rite, which caused me intermittent anxiety. Soon after arriving in Caerleon, I'd become friends with Andrea, largely due to her house being on the same road. It came to pass that

Andrea had in her possession certain leaflets regarding the onset of menstruation, of which, at the ripe old age of nearly eleven, I knew not a thing so it was lucky it hadn't struck me early. One rainy afternoon, she took me in hand and taught me the lot in a nutshell or, shall we say, a bombshell. I was stunned. She also showed me her favourite leaflet in her collection, which dealt with how babies come about—another shocker. I tried to erase the contents of this leaflet from my mind as the thought of the oncoming menstrual tide was already enough to deal with in one day. In any case, I was certain I would never become pregnant so it wouldn't affect me. A dog would suffice for my offspring.

When menstruation caught up with me two years later, I was embarrassed when I told my mother, hesitantly describing the vaguest of symptoms. On her way out to work, she presented me with a packet of superfluously gigantic sanitary towels that hampered my walking. I felt quite miserable about a future involving colossal sanitary towels. I was given the day off school but felt normal. Now and again, I checked the mirror for signs that I'd reached womanhood but saw none. My reflection revealed only a girl in a nightdress who was feeling fine. The sick note I handed to my form teacher the next day explained I'd had a 'stomach ache', the codename of the past for all things menstrual. Hard on the heels of menstruation came the sprouting of further mortifying signs of maturity, leading me to avail surreptitiously of my father's razor from time to time. He was baffled as to why it often seemed rather blunt.

During that first summer with Andrea in Caerleon, before the encumbrances of puberty, I showed off to her a little by climbing a tree, but lost my footing and tumbled down. There were other children nearby who ran over to see what had happened. Clutching the back of my head, I rushed to my house and shut the door before bursting into tears where no one could witness it. Minutes later, I went completely blind and stopped crying in shock. No one was home so I slowly felt my way upstairs to my room and lay down, thinking it would eventually pass like the migraine headaches I got from my food allergies. If I blinked hard, I could see for a second. When my mother came home from work, I told her I had a headache, embarrassed by my predicament. The next day, waking up with normal sight, I mentioned in passing to my mother that I had been blind for much of the previous day. She took me to see the doctor who tested my reflexes with a rubber hammer and told me I'd been a lucky girl.

There was a mental hospital nearby with wooded grounds in which Andrea and I enjoyed the thrill of stalking around. On one occasion, a huge and dishevelled man popped out from behind a tree and asked us the time, which was the most excitement we'd had in a long while. We took to going to church on Sunday mornings as patients from the mental hospital would often be there and we had developed a weird fascination for them. We were, by far, the youngest members of the elderly and dwindling congregation. It was splendid when, one Sunday, a lady stood up in the middle of the posh old vicar's sermon and shouted out that her 'drawers' were cleaner than his. Was she delusional or did she know something that we didn't?

During this same summer when I turned eleven, I saw my first corpse, albeit in pieces. Next to the mental hospital was a bridge over some railway tracks. Andrea and I would cross this bridge when we walked down into the centre of Caerleon where, being idle children, we'd buy iced buns from the bakery, eat them on the village green and then amble back home again. There were a handful of foolhardy youngsters who, like us, had nothing to do over the summer holidays. They showed off by walking on top of the bridge's fence on a foot wide riveted steel girder. Andrea and I could barely look. Crossing the bridge one day, we paused as there were a number of policemen in high visibility jackets on the track. Andrea called down to ask what had happened and a policeman put the 'mind your own business' finger to his nose. We did not and continued to watch. Ten minutes later, a strangely Dickensian scene unfolded before us. Four under-takers in black tailcoats and top hats with black ribbons came into view. They were making their way tentatively down the track carrying an elaborate coffin on their shoulders. At a certain spot, they put it on the ground and then began filling it with lumps they were finding scattered about. When they had finished, they screwed down the lid, but they couldn't lift it up onto their shoulders, however hard they tried. They finally solved this problem by sliding the coffin along the rail of the tracks.

We spent a week wondering which of the reck-lessly brave youths it could have been. Then a little notice appeared in the local paper saying that a patient from the mental hospital had taken his life on the railway track. The picture showed the big man who had come out from behind the tree and asked us the time.

The summer holiday ended and Andrea and I walked down to school on the first day, speculating nervously about how they would do the cold bath. I was certain they'd put us in the same class to be nice as I knew no one else. Hundreds of children in their new uniforms stood in the assembly hall to be sorted into three groups, which we gradually understood were, in a basic sense, clever, average and special educational needs. To my horror, Andrea left me, summoned to the clever stream. I was then corralled among the average joes as, in batches of thirty, we were deposited into different form rooms. A couple of quieter girls, Ruth and Kate, felt my pain and clustered around me. We were classmates for the next three years and there was no cold bath.

Ruth and Kate could not have been from more different backgrounds yet they would be close right through their school years, united mainly through shyness in public, but with an underlying quiet confidence within their social circle. Ruth's parents owned the village bakery and her family lived in a small mansion filled with gleaming antiques. Their wealth was founded on people like me with sugar addictions who were repeatedly drawn to their bakery. The French windows that opened onto the smooth lawns were usually ajar, their delicate muslin rippling in the breeze. On the other end of the spectrum, Kate lived in her grandmother's threadbare council house with her divorced father and two younger siblings. Her friendly grandmother, a round, hunched lady had only two front teeth which stayed outside her mouth when it was closed. Until I visited Kate's, I had no idea about coin-operated electricity meters, nor had I ever experienced scrambling around for a fifty pence piece in the pitch dark.

I may have been in the average joes but I doubted the basic intelligence of a number of my peers. In a pair-work exercise in English, we were asked to put things on a list in order of importance for an astronaut. I had the most exasperating argument of my life with a pale, blonde boy, who was almost see-through, as his name, Kenneth Window, suggested. Window insisted a hot drink go at the top of the list before oxygen. My 'How can he drink if he can't breathe?' fell upon deaf ears. I can still remember the teacher's bemused expression when he jumped in to tell her what *we* had decided, to my mortified embarrassment.

I gradually got into the swing of 'big school', mainly taking an interest in history, English and art. My favourite teacher was Mr. Hawker to whom I attribute, amongst other things, the revelation of my first naked man. Mr. Hawker was more than a teacher; he was a highly accomplished painter with portraits in art galleries, who'd had a long career as an artist. He was at the school only for a few months, covering for the regular teacher's maternity leave. One day, he brought in a collection of large photographs of his work. The third one he held up, a full-length, full-frontal male nude, plunged the class into a stunned silence. I remember the face of the man in the portrait, framed by long wavy hair, his expression distant. 'He paid me to do this life-size portrait of him,' Mr. Hawker told us, 'Then he never collected it. Six months later his family came for it as he had died. He had planned it, you see, as a gift to them, to remember him by.' Mr. Hawker liked to share his art tricks, such as spreading out the bristles of the brush to paint grass. He demonstrated little bits on our canvases, then scolded himself as, he said, he didn't want to be grading his own work.

There were also easy subjects which I didn't mind, like religious education, where a typical lesson would be something like 'Draw and Label the Ziggurat of Ur'. Our teacher, Miss Plumpton was a wholesome, curly-haired woman who couldn't pronounce the letter R so it was, accordingly, a source of amusement to us to get her to repeat the phrase, 'Ziggurat of Ur'. She had congealed mascara that intrigued me, especially when a globule of it once landed on my exercise book and I poked it with the point of my pencil. In R.E., I came to comprehend the ubiquitous popularity of chips among my peers when, during our first lesson, Miss Plumpton, asked us what kinds of journeys we made in our lives and several boys offered 'Going for chips'. She refined their responses with 'Yes, a journey to find food', which she duly related to various Biblical tales, such as Joseph's brothers journeying to Egypt during the seven lean years of famine.

I soon took to making my own Biblical journeys to find food at lunchtimes in an effort to avoid the canteen's soggy fare. Going off campus was permitted but considered a little risqué, something only slightly wild pupils did. I certainly wasn't wild, but following along with the wilder types was an interesting new experience. The sensible Ruth and Kate stayed behind in the school canteen that smelled of Shepherd's Pie, whilst I sprang out of the school gates with Andrea and her bold friends from the clever stream. We'd make a beeline for the chippy, which was manned by a group of young Chinese men all of whom used to shout across to each other in Cantonese when I entered, down frying tools and stare, clearly enamoured by my porcelain complexion, pigtails and whatever was starting to bubble under my school blouse. To the consternation of the others, I always received extra chips and a flirtatious scattering of batter scraps, intended perhaps to hasten my development.

A desire to engage in a spot of naughty behaviour was frequently the real reason to go off campus at lunchtimes. One of Andrea's friends from her clever class, Liz, was experimenting with a career in shoplifting, befitting a girl of presumably high intellect. It didn't look at all clever to me though. In fact, it was downright miserable as she would 'because she could' steal things like a mini-bottle of cherryade from a down-at-heel little sweet shop owned by a kindly old lady, or a packet of clothes pegs from a scrappy homewares stall run by an impoverished couple. I always hoped Liz wouldn't be joining us but Andrea seemed enthralled with her.

Another lunchtime jaunt was going to the ancient Roman amphitheatre near the school, which happened to be free of charge. It gained in popularity and soon hordes of adolescents from the school were swarming over its Roman paving and racing up and down its grassy banks. A phone call was made to the headmaster, Wallis Simpson, as he was known, for what reason I never learned. He marched over to the amphitheatre one lunchtime, with what was left of his hair swirling around his face like a storm cloud and dispersed the gathering the moment he came into view. He then sent letters home urging parents to get their children school dinners or provide a packed lunch.

My mother told me to buy the school dinner and I agreed to this, although I had other plans. We did not venture to the amphitheatre again but we continued to patronise the chip shop. This had now become difficult for me, however, as my mother had asked her retired friend, Edna to watch out for me over the lunch break. She'd met Edna through the Women's Institute and, discovering that she had a bungalow on Cold Bath Road, had enlisted her services. Edna or, as I began to refer to her, 'Evil Edna' (after a witch in the shape of a television in a children's cartoon), was always vigilant at her window when I happened to be passing, so that I had to place myself in the middle of an especially dense gaggle to escape her eagle eye.

A weekly event in one of the morning breaks was the hurling of a certain small boy into the long jump sandpit. The cry of 'They're chucking Oscar!' caused a stampede, not only because it was fascinating to see a boy sail high through the air, but because the fifth-formers were trying to break their record. I wasn't sure whether Oscar Bloom was willing or not, but he never showed any resistance. He landed with reasonable grace and the larger boys recorded their throw with a tape measure whilst he brushed the sand from his trousers and swiftly walked off. He never seemed to have any expression and his large nose and glasses looked like the Groucho Marx masks you got in joke shops, only without the black plastic moustache.

Despite being boldly energetic at home, a tree climber, an accomplished tag player and a coverer of vast distances with my dog, I was not one of the chosen ones in sport. The one time I represented the school in hockey, last minute because someone was ill, in an away match against a team infamous for their robust players, I threw down my stick and ran off the pitch when a herd of girls started eagerly pursuing me and the ball. The skeletal and always tanned Miss Horsham shook her head from the sidelines and swore never to put the likes of me in a match again.

The other girls' sports teacher, Miss Evans, was opposite in appearance to her colleague, squat, pale and round. She was constantly trying to sort out our running form, which she described in her Welsh accent as 'flailing'. On one occasion, she was giving us yet another of her expert demos in the usual way, jogging on the spot, her stubby arms moving like little pistons, when a cricket ball from the boys' lesson at the other end of the field sailed in a wide arc across the sky and came to an abrupt halt on the top of her head. We watched in wonder as she continued to jog for a few more seconds before dropping unconscious to the ground.

The alarming practice of having to stand naked in the communal shower after our weekly sports lesson mortified many of us so we developed a system to avoid it. While the sports teachers were supervising the collection of equipment, we would sprint to the changing rooms faster than we'd ever run in the sports lesson. When we got there, we would briskly get out of our sports kit and into our uniforms, after which we'd dampen our hair in the sink to create the illusion of having showered. Once, a rather dopey girl copied us and almost rumbled our ruse. One of the sports teachers returned and told her to have a shower and she said she'd had one, indicating her wet hair. In response, the sports teacher asked her why then was she still in her sports kit? We had to be extra cautious after that. At risk, however, were those who were chosen to carry the equipment in from the sports field so one had to make sure to be out of range when the time came for the two teachers to make that selection. These ill-starred carriers would then have to shower with all of us dressed ones trying not to look, but occasionally glancing, inwardly agog, at bodies that were all-too-rapidly becoming those of women.

3

Fruitful Lessons in Home Economy

My worst performance was in the 'girls' subjects' of needlework and home economics. I found threading the sewing machine baffling and the noisy jabbing needle alarming. On one occasion, I almost sewed a button onto my thumb. I'd spend months on a garment and the only item I remember ever completing, a crimson nightshirt in a rough synthetic material, fell to pieces the first night I wore it.

Home economics should have been called cookery for that was all it was. Just walking into that classroom was difficult for me because I'd always had an uneasy relationship with food. Much of it gave me the worst kind of nauseous migraine headaches that didn't stop until I vomited whatever had brought them on. My mother would try to induce this dramatic finale by giving me salt water in a plastic cup but it only made matters worse. The main things I felt safe about eating were toast with peanut butter or bread with the peculiar Sandwich Spread, diced vegetables in mayonnaise, or 'sick in a jar' as we referred to it.

A typical meal at home was steak and kidney pie with a filling flecked with carrots that oozed out from under a gravy-logged pastry top. The heady bouquet was more than I could bear yet I was under a curse to finish everything on my plate. I would fake cough into my hand and surreptitiously transfer the revolting morsels into the napkin on my lap, which I would later deposit into the dog's bowl.

My parents would retire to the sitting room to watch the news, to which I would listen tensely through the louvre doors, forgetting the food in front of me. Some of the frequent topics haunted my childhood and even seeped into my dreams: nuclear missiles, the warzone in Northern Ireland which I knew wasn't far away, the despot Idi Amin with his exaggerated frogging and rows of shiny medals and 'The Basque separatist group, ETA' interpreted by me as 'vast separatist', which confused me further. I understood that the 'group' was based in far off Spain but still, the stern expressions of the dark-haired 'ETA people' in their televised mugshots, always unsettled me. In those days, the bleak news was often rounded off with an uplifting story, usually involving a baby animal, such as the birth of a fuzzy new panda with a rhyming Chinese name, but it didn't fool even a child. We knew we'd been born into a fractured world.

Meanwhile, sentry-like, my parents took it in turns to observe me through the slots in the louvre doors, ready with volleys of berating if I paused in eating. Mushy carrots would make my mouth spasm into an involuntary gape, like the skeleton in an urn burial that had recently transfixed me in a school history book. My father would tell me to 'Cut it out!' but I had no control over it and, more often than not, it was a foreshadowing that the food was going to make me enormously ill.

On the other hand, even food that tasted wonderful sometimes did that in the aftermath. Against my better judgement, I'd once wolfed a slice of delicious cherry pie. That night, due to the unusual angle of my face as I slept, I'd vomited it up the wall. The line of pink stayed there permanently, blending in loosely with the carnation print wallpaper. There was another stain on the edge of a circular rug in the hallway, a result of my scoffing a cocktail glass of butterscotch Angel Delight garnished with a glace cherry. It was fortunate the rug happened to be woven, unusually for a design with roses, in russet hues. Easter was always a difficult time, with the alluring smell of chocolate in the houses of other children. I'd learned my lesson after sneakily downing half a chocolate egg at a friend's and crashing into a door from the dazzling lights of the migraine that had ensued. I was sent home after that, under suspicion of having been at their drinks cabinet.

Given the lack of variety in the meal repertoire at home, I'd get so hungry that I'd offer to clean the car for fifty pence in order to blow the lot on sweets at the corner shop. I knew what would turn my stomach so I avoided the spongy sweets in shrimp and banana shapes, along with the Bakelite bar of Caramac. The necklaces threaded with chalky, pastel-coloured sweets were fun to gnaw on but they made my neck sticky and, as the custom at home was to bathe but once a week, this could be uncomfortable. Sherbet fountains and white chocolate mice likewise elicited no adverse reaction.

As a small child, I remember being drawn to the idea of making food, perhaps as some kind of attempt to take control and censor the ingredients. All my endeavors, alas, were ill-fated. On one occasion, I amassed some pastry offcuts, which I rolled out and stamped into star shapes. There was soil under my nails from an earlier al fresco culinary venture making mud pies in the garden, which had made the pastry turn grey as I squeezed it into a ball. Despite their being on the grimy side, my 'biscuits' were baked and slipped onto a saucer before my father at the dinner table. As he read *The Daily Mail*, oblivious to their greyish hue, he consumed the lot, at which my mother had raised a wry eyebrow.

Once I started at the comprehensive, I'd brace myself for the fortnightly cookery practicals which always seemed to go wrong for me. I probably should have entered May's pantry more frequently to learn the mystical ways of baking. I lumbered along, carrying my ingredients the two miles to school in the obligatory wicker basket that bumped against my knees, puckered and red because I could never get my socks to stay up. I was a good girl who would never vulgarly eat what I'd made as I walked home, like I'd seen others doing, with chocolate mousse and such like smeared all over their hands. No, I wanted to impress my mother with what I'd created, but all too frequently, I returned home with an empty basket after yet another gastronomic disaster.

Mrs Shackleton, the Scottish home economics teacher, was an older lady in an apple-dappled nylon housecoat that served to enhance the classroom's fruity colour palette of lemon formica worktops and lime green lino flooring. She ran a tight ship, with the saucepans polished mirror-bright and utensils organized alphabetically. Pink-rimmed spectacles were balanced on her bony nose, their thick lenses magnifying her eyes to give her a look of perpetual enthusiasm, right from our first lesson: 'We'll start off with something easy, girls...jelly!' Everyone else had brought in neat little round jelly moulds but all I could find at home was a foot long mould in the shape of a carp. With the grace of an inexperienced tightrope walker, I edged toward the fridge with my brimming carp, but suddenly and inexplicably found myself splayed on the lino, my school uniform coated in half-set jelly. I lay there a while, amid the tepid gelatinousness, in the thrall of a nauseous wave. 'Disaster Girl!' Mrs Shackleton had shrieked and the accolade had stuck for good reason.

The next assignment was mashed potatoes but I hadn't thought to add water, and stood wondering why everyone else was at the mashing stage when I was still waiting for the potatoes to become soft in the saucepan. Mrs Shackleton's nostrils soon sourced the singeing smell but by then there was nothing to be done. 'Surely everyone knows what boiling is!' Mrs Shackleton announced mainly to me, 'Do I really have to say 'boil the potatoes in water', rather than just 'boil the potatoes'?'

I walked home empty-handed again, taunted by popular girls behind me...'Disaster Girl strikes again! Destroying all food in her path!' They were right. Like King Midas, any food I touched was turned into something inedible, only it wasn't pretty like gold.

On Pancake Day, I accidentally brought in self-raising flour when it was 'essential', Mrs Shackleton reiterated, that one's pancakes 'turn out no thicker than a swatch of velvet, girls'. Mine were the thickness of corrugated cardboard and, since I had also forgotten to add sugar, of a similar flavour too.

Scotch Eggs were the next disaster. I'd had a promising start, hard boiling the eggs in water and seasoning the sausagemeat while I waited. 'Now, girls, when your egg timer goes off, plunge your eggs into icy cold water to eschew a nasty green yolk,' Mrs Shackleton warned from the front.

I was sharing a table with Ruth, who always had her hair neatly tied back on cooking days in a crocheted band she'd made herself. As her parents owned the village bakery, there was always fresh bread at her house which I'd never had before and found astounding. On my first visit, I devoured the best part of a loaf, whilst her mother looked on compassionately. Ruth was already poised to take over the family business within the next decade, and was quietly absorbed in culinary perfectionism, folding her microscopically chopped parsley into the pink, fluffy sausagemeat. When the egg timer went off and Ruth stood up to take her eggs off the heat and douse them in cold water, I did the same. Together we peeled our eggs and began wrapping the sausagemeat around them, a fiddly process. I gripped one of my eggs a little too forcefully and my stomach churned when an ooze of yellow yolk seeped out.

'You didn't boil them long enough,' Ruth declared matter-of-factly, 'You took them off when you heard my egg timer because you forgot yours at home.'

I did my best to tentatively pat the sausagemeat, which had now become distinctly gooier, into place around my deflated egg, overcome by queasiness.

Mrs Shackleton made another announcement from the front, 'Once you've rolled your sausaged egg in the breadcrumbs, girls, ensure that the oil in your deep-fat fryer is scalding hot before immersing your eggs using the wire basket.'

When I saw the oil starting to bubble, I dropped in my Scotch Eggs. It was all going so well apart from the minor mishap earlier. I watched my bona fide Scotch Eggs rolling around in the boiling oil at the bottom of the saucepan but, oh dear, they were starting to bump into each other and the breadcrumbs were falling away in large flakes. I saw Ruth remove her eggs in one fell swoop with a deft movement of her wire basket. Ah, the wire basket! I'd just put mine in loose and they were plainly doomed, whereas Ruth's hadn't lost a breadcrumb and were, as Mrs Shackleton pertly observed, 'uniformly golden and perfectly spherical'.

'How do I get them out if I put them in loose?' I asked Ruth, hoping she didn't think me too much of an imbecile. She was too deeply absorbed in arranging her eggs on a rustic board with wafer thin gherkin slices to answer me straight away. She sliced one of the eggs in half and propped it up at a shop-window angle ready to receive top marks.

'You could try a slotted spoon,' she finally suggested with a discernible sigh.

I rushed to the utensil drawer labelled S and tried to think which implement there might be a slotted spoon. By the time I'd selected it and returned, my eggs had blackened on the outside. Still, I arranged them on a plate, sawed one in half and propped it up on a chunk of cucumber.

'You appear to have lost your yolk,' was Mrs Shackleton's laconic judgement as she noted my mark in her book.

I took them home all the same, picked the burnt bits off and put them on a plate on the table where my mother likened them to the frightful rock cakes of her spinster aunt.

The final cookery class of the year involved Mrs Shackleton's demo on how to make the perfect Victoria Sandwich, which we were to replicate at home and bring in for the school competition. She cut the finished cake up into tiny triangles and each of us got to sample a sliver of the perfect sponge.

I tried to fix in my mind the exact hue of pale yellow the butter and sugar turned when the creaming was complete, and sought to learn by heart Mrs Shackleton's admonition that it was, 'Tantamount to sacrilege to tip the sponge domed side down onto the cooling rack first as it would thereby become blemished with an ugly lattice, thrown into sharp relief once dusted with icing sugar.'

No one was in the house on the evening I made my Victoria Sandwich. I turned on the fluorescent light in the kitchen and found a cookbook in the drawer, something May had given to my mother. The paper had worn thin on the pages of favourite recipes including the Victoria Sandwich. A colony of silverfish had taken up residence in the forgotten cake tins under the oven. Only two tins matched but, getting out my school ruler, I found they were exactly the right measurement for the recipe so I tipped out the silverfish and gave the tins a rinse. I weighed the ingredients three times to make sure I had it right, and found just enough raspberry jam in the bottom of a jar for the filling. While the cake baked, I crouched on the kitchen floor and stared through the oven door window watching it swell up. Later, as the two halves sat on the cooling rack, I was astonished to see that they'd risen beautifully and were a perfect cakey brown.

I carried the assembled sponge to school the next morning in a Tupperware container inside my wicker basket, and dropped it off in the room set aside for the cake competition. Victoria Sandwiches of multifarious shapes and sizes lined every surface. I found that overnight I'd developed a discerning eye as 'the faults' in many of the others jumped out at me: that one didn't have the domed side facing up, this one had the dread marks of the cooling rack upon it, someone had even forgotten the baking powder and had basically made a jam-filled frisbee.

Ruth strolled in and set down the largest and most miraculous Victoria Sandwich I had ever laid eyes upon right in the middle of the room. It was on a blue china plate, perfectly domed and dusted. 'That's a nice little one,' she said with a tinge of surprise when she noticed mine, 'Don't forget to write your name on a scrap of paper and stick it under the plate.'

At the end of the day, I went to collect my cake. It was one of twenty or so that had a little slice cut out of them and I was thrilled to realise it had got through the first test. 'The Victoria Sandwich must have a pleasing appearance, girls,' Mrs Shackleton had said, and the judges were only going to sample those cakes that met this criteria. I couldn't see any rosette on the winning cake. It must have been taken away already and, as Ruth's had gone, I concluded that it was the likely winner.

I carried my sponge back home and placed it in the middle of the dining room table. I had made it all by myself and it contained no ingredients that turned my stomach. I had followed the recipe correctly and hadn't dropped or burnt anything. It was a perfect cake.

The meal that evening—broiled liver with a topping of overly sauteed onions—was made slightly less unbearable with the wonderful dessert to look forward to. My father even indulged me in a moment of rare praise, saying my cake was excellent and should have won. I was no longer Disaster Girl and my baking prowess prompted Ruth to invite me round to her house again for more fresh bread and to see some kittens.

In the library a fortnight later, I overheard a group of girls asking Mrs Shackleton whose cake had won the competition. I expected to hear Ruth's name but instead was stunned to hear my own, followed by Mrs Shackleton's expostulating that it had been 'Most unexpected!' when she had seen my name on the slip of paper under the plate.

Following this, I became consistently adequate in cookery classes, but with some excellent peaks such as a distinctive Fruit Fool. Mrs Shackleton was at last able to relax when I walked into the room. I became a high flyer in other subjects too and suddenly excellent in French following my first evertrip abroad to the Loire Valley, where my father had, quite inexplicably, splashed out on a foreign holiday. Miraculously, none of the French food made me ill. I had no idea a soup made from potatoes could taste so marvellous. The simple act of asking for bread and cakes, fruit and vegetables in the little French shops made my confidence in speaking another language blossom. There was even talk among the teachers of elevating me to the clever pupils' sphere until, quite suddenly, I had to leave that school.

4

How to Survive in Hostile Climes

'The wheel arches are a bit low, aren't they?' my father observed. Of course they were, we had loaded most of our possessions into the back of my mother's Mini Clubman and were leaving the marital home. She had covered the lot with a groundsheet and placed Jess, the golden retriever, on top as a distraction.

'It'll be okay. Ta-ta!' my mother smiled as she drove off, waving goodbye to a twenty-five-year-long marriage. We were headed north to Whitehaven for what he thought was a week-long holiday, but which we knew was permanent.

A week before, my mother had said to me in the kitchen, 'You don't like your father, do you?' It was hard to answer as he'd been warm-hearted when I was small, lifting me up to the ceiling when he came home from work, but as I'd grown into an older, more questioning child who was not so easy to lift up, his interest had waned. Pretty much the only words he said to me now were to be quiet when he was watching sport on the television, usually with his stock phrase, 'Get back in your box!'.

I was ambivalent. On the one hand, I wanted to

stay in the school where I was comfortable and had friends. On the other, I was keen to see more of Manda, the only person in my life who was physically affectionate. My parents hadn't been this way for years so I'd grown used to the lack of it and was accustomed to it, although I did experience a pleasing tingle whenever Manda gave me a hug. Perhaps my parents had an old-fashioned idea that one had to be emotionally self-sufficient from an early age, a notion particularly pertinent to my mother who'd lost her father so young. Fourteen would be our mutual age for losing our fathers, only for her it had been literal and devastating.

While I possibly disliked my father, neither could I say I was close to my mother. I saw little of either of them because, when I wasn't in school, I'd trawl about the neighbourhood with the dog or with other children, often staying out until dark. My sisters had left home before I was twelve, one to study law at university and the other to become an air traffic controller in the military. My mother told me it had been her intention to wait until I'd left home too before she ended the marriage but she couldn't cope with living with my father any longer. She had hidden the extent of her unhappiness for a long time and I felt sorry for her. I went along with the plan numbly, taking care to say nothing to my father, as instructed by my mother, and suspecting that if I raised an objection, it would change nothing.

We would be staying at May's and, to my relief, I wouldn't be sleeping on the camp-bed in the corner of her room. A bed was made up for me, in the parlour, of all places. Cumbria was colder than

South Wales so I was given a small electric heater for use in the evenings only.

The next day, my mother and I went over to Manda and Wiff's and she announced, quite proudly, that she'd left their son but hadn't got around to telling him yet. They were thunderstruck, their old jaws dropped and I remember wishing she'd delivered the news more gently but then, she had been unhappily married for a couple of decades and was feeling liberated, throwing caution to the wind.

Wiff left the house abruptly and marched down to the phone box on the corner to inform his son of the news. There were strong reasons why she hadn't wanted to tell my father face to face. He was a hot-tempered fellow and their rows, usually over modest household bills, sometimes ended with her in tears. He earned a large salary and spent most of it on himself. She had to work as a secretary so she wouldn't have to ask him for life's necessities, with her wages covering all our clothes, food and bills.

Whenever my father returned from business trips, I hung around while he unpacked his case because he often had some bits and bobs from his hotel room which he'd give me: little soaps, a miniature toothpaste, a comb in a paper sleeve. Once he brought back some American chewing gum from his trip to San Francisco. Christmas was a time of frugality and I was puzzled by other parents' largesse towards their children. My single gift from my parents, or rather from my mother as she chose and paid for it, was always limited to something practical, generally an item of clothing. This didn't really bother me because I knew which neighbouring child to call on when I fancied playing with a certain toy. My mother regarded bicycles as dangerous but there were various ones I could lay my hands on for a few hours without her knowledge. Once I received a wristwatch from my parents and, on another auspicious Yuletide, a digital alarm clock. Time was an important theme to my mother as she was acutely aware that too much of it had been wasted married to my father.

My mother was having interviews for secretarial jobs in Whitehaven and I had a couple of days to spare before I started at my new school so I wandered about the town centre on my own. This was something I'd never done on our short visits when I was younger and these wanderings would become an absorbing pastime for the next few years.

On this first perambulation, it dawned on me that Whitehaven was the land that time forgot. The epicentre of the town was a forlorn harbour, dotted with neglected boats keeling over in foul-smelling mud. It was strange to think that, back in the 1700s, this was the second busiest port in England, which had led to Whitehaven becoming a wealthy town with an abundance of impressive town houses. All that had now dwindled to a scattering of small pubs and just two shopping streets, with many of the old houses in various stages of disrepair and the harbour used only by local fishermen. The town centre was largely haunted by old men in trenchcoats, flat caps and, more often than not, walking retired grey-hounds on plaited rope leads. They'd call across the road to clones of themselves 'Ow yer doin', marra?' or even just 'Ow do, marra?', 'marra' being Cumbrian dialect for 'friend', as in someone who is so close to you that they are like marrow, or 'marra', in your bones. The typical reply would be 'As alreet, pal, ow's thu?'. If someone had addressed you as 'marra', that word was now taken and you had to reply to them as 'pal'.

Most of the shops had been there for decades, like the drapers, for example, with its curved glass windows and long wooden counter where they'd measure out the cloth. I would often browse in Michael Moon's labyrinthine antiquarian bookshop, more recent but old fashioned in style. Another shop, and I use the term loosely here, consisted of a knee-high heap of bric-a-brac, everything from rusty spanners to dolls' legs, presided over by one of the old trenchcoat fellows, a cigarette in his yellowed fingers, sitting on a camping chair. People would occasionally venture inside and, with the toe of a shoe, nudge the pile around until they found something they fancied. The proprietor would name a price but it was often too high as he was a reluctant retailer who seemed to have grown attached to his chattels.

Along with the old men in trenchcoats, there were a few other characters who stood out and whom I invariably saw on visits to the town centre. There was the ginger-haired man, with his drooping moustache, always in light, hippyish clothes, whatever the weather. He had a laid back way of strolling, as if going nowhere in particular, and always smiled at me in a faraway manner. When I returned to the town a few years ago, he was still there, still underdressed, although his hair had turned grey. He smiled at me in the same way and I wondered whether he recognised me, or if it was just his standard smile for everyone.

Another town centre character was a drunken sot who perpetually grinned, but at no one because his eyes were blank. He would sit on a bench in the grounds of the ruined Saint Nicholas church, his black hair sweat-plastered to his head. Worse though, was the sight of his very elderly mother who rushed about, surprisingly nimble, looking for him about the town. She had a face like a crumpled dish cloth and carried a bag clinking with bottles. I didn't know what was going on but I presumed it was her aim to keep him in his stupefied state lest he turn from comatose to disorderly. I stopped seeing them after a couple of years and presumed they'd both gone to their graves.

I went shopping with my mother for the navy blue and white uniform of Richmond School. I preferred the warmer colours of burgundy and pale blue, the uniform at my last school. Richmond was housed in the former grammar school building, where my parents had spent the latter half of their school days, albeit in different classes. My mother's opinion of my father was that he was a loud, disruptive boy so it was mystifying that they had got together in their late teens, which had led to an unexpected pregnancy and the, then unavoidable swift marriage.

The entrance at Richmond opened into the assembly hall, with its well-trodden parquet floor and a sagging minstrel's gallery along one side. Doors to classrooms were straight off the hall. It was on a much smaller scale than my previous school and thoroughly dilapidated. I was taken to a strangely sparse classroom with shabby wainscoting. Dwindling numbers should probably have served as a warning sign to my mother and the more modern school up the hill ought to have been investigated, but that would have been another story and probably a dull, predictable one.

A few more things at Richmond struck me as odd almost immediately. It was the 1980s yet most of the girls in my year had names belonging to a former age: Dorothy, Millicent, Eileen, Margaret, Rosemary, Dora. The shoes and coats they were wearing with their uniforms in the chilly classrooms had a pre-war look to them. Oddest of all, however, was the way they spoke which I could barely fathom. This was curious because I'd always understood my grandparents perfectly well when we came over for visits. I soon learned that this was the more slack-jawed, less enunciated, monotone strain of the local accent used by the roughest of Cumbrian youth.

'Brian-sez-thoos-fyas-is-bonny,' Margaret nudged me on my second day. 'Fyas' meant face and 'thoos' was a corruption of the archaic thine combined with thou. 'Wi'thee-gowi'him?' she continued. I found it strange that their dialect also featured 'thee' making them sound like coarser Shakespearean characters.

'Go with him where?' I didn't know that this was a version of 'go out with' as in become a girl/boyfriend. Everyone laughed raucously.

'Spewsy-wans-hertogo-wi'*im!*' Dorothy chimed in. Spewsy, a sickly-looking, corpulent boy, put his head under his anorak.

'Go where?' I asked again. More jarring laughter

at my clipped tones since I'd never lived in a place long enough to properly pick up a local accent.

'Brian-wansababby-wi'yer!' Dorothy was on a roll.

My parents hadn't intentionally 'kept me from children who were rough', it was just that I'd never encountered them in such concentration before and it was fairly overwhelming.

After a week of this banter, they didn't find me entertaining any more. Too many of the boys had come clean and said they did want to 'go with' me, after the girls had forced them to confess at compass point. I was now seen as a threat to the future pro-creation of the Cumbrian race. The boys were dopey but most of the girls turned on me with rancour, culminating in Dorothy's stuffing a fistful of soil into my 'posh' mouth. I ran away gagging and spitting the stuff out, which had the desired effect as many of the boys witnessed this and recoiled.

'Yera-who-er!' Dorothy howled after me, which word was later translated for me as whore.

Apart from the large group of delinquent girls, who got away with the majority of their distasteful acts as the teachers were cowed, there were other sub-groups. I stuck to a couple of calmer girls, Carol and Rachel, who kept their heads down and steered clear of the barbarity, carefully choosing where they sat in the classrooms and avoiding hostile territory at breaktimes. During lunch we'd huddle together in a corner over the only meal the canteen offered, chips and beans. Though the school was awful, I had to admit the chips were excellent, consistently light brown and crispy on the outside yet soft and light on the inside. Likewise, the only dessert on offer was homemade caramel shortbread and it still holds its place as the best caramel shortbread I've ever had. Unfortunately, the dinner ladies never made enough of it. I once inadvertently took the last piece and had to keep far away from Dorothy for the rest of the week.

There was another group, a handful of children who were totally bewildered in a school where there appeared to be no provision for them. Dean Crab was a diminutive boy with a square head, a huge hearing aid and small eyes that were unnaturally far apart, like a crab's, fittingly. The delinquents used to say he'd been 'runover-byabus'. He sat at the back of classes, where the teachers would give him some paper to doodle on. Some of the crueler pupils enjoyed chasing him around at breaktimes.

One day, Dean brought a large, threadbare teddy to school. He was left in peace to sit with it on his lap during morning classes but at lunchtime Millicent snatched it away and the dreadful girl gang tossed it back and forth over his head while he leapt feebly a few inches off the ground trying to catch it, letting forth dissonant moans. I desperately wanted to put a stop to this torment but, to my shame, I was too afraid. Eventually, the teddy was torn open at the neck, its stuffing tumbling out and scattering around the school yard. Millicent tossed the deflated plush corpse onto the tarmac and Dean, with his equally ragged and stunted twin sister, Rosemary, scampered about trying to gather up the spindrift foam. They had no coats and their hands were blue with cold.

Rosemary, though not hard of hearing, also

couldn't follow the lessons. As a matter of fact, I had trouble too. Most of the teachers had no plans and would frequently leave their classrooms for lengthy stretches. When the Crab twins left school at sixteen, Rosemary took to playing bingo alongside Manda most afternoons at the pensioners' hut in Hensingham. Manda told me Rosemary liked to swig from a bottle of milk as she ticked off her numbers.

Classes at Richmond were generally turbulent. The geography teacher, who doubled as the deputy head, would hastily select a page number from a tattered textbook which would be a tedious bit of reading on something like arable farming in Gloucestershire, followed by some boring questions. He would then leave us to it, going off on deputy head business. Naturally, no one did a thing as he never checked our books. There was a lot of graffiti in the textbooks, some of it dating back twenty years, which made the content somewhat irrelevant.

The English teacher, Mrs. Kay, a well-meaning southerner with chubby red cheeks and a jolly manner, didn't fully understand the northern children before her but I now suspect she knew they were wild and likely to fall pregnant at any moment. Probably for this reason, she chose to teach Stan Barstow's *A Kind of Loving*, in which a working class northern man tries to better himself but gets a girl pregnant, causing his plans to go pear-shaped and dashing his prospects. We read snippets in class and watched the TV adaptation. Sadly, it was all lost on Millicent who left school a few months later at the age of fifteen, to 'ha'e-ababby', which I feared might soon go the way of Dean or his teddy, unless it were immediately put up for adoption.

As I had recently risen to the top of the class in French at my last school, I looked forward to my first French lesson at Richmond. Mr. Ball, however, played to the delinquents and his first interaction with me was to make me ask for a sanitary towel in French. Thereafter, I knew it would be a lesson I would dread. He was a vain fellow who enjoyed babbling about croissants and escargot and all the other French food he'd had on his frequent trips over the Channel, all quite lost on the insular mob before him. I have to say that I received more than a modicum of satisfaction when I saw Mr. Ball, three years later, after Richmond had been closed and razed to the ground, trawling around the biscuit aisle of the Spar mini-market, leaning heavily on his trolley which contained nothing but an unimpressive packet of Rich Tea Fingers, his once flounced hair now lank and greasy.

In this barren learning environment, there was one bright spark, the history teacher, Mrs. Galley, an elfin, golden-skinned older lady, always dressed in an A-line skirt, tidy blouse and flat shoes. It astonished me how she could hold the rabble in the palm of her hand as she told stories of the two World Wars whilst standing in the middle of the classroom, clear, expressive and gesticulating dramatically. The following year, when that class sat and failed the majority of their final exams, history was one of the only subjects a handful of them passed.

Meanwhile, life at Hilltop Road had taken a downward turn. My mother's much older brother, Jim, was grumbling about our presence. Jim, now in his sixties, had never left home and was a miserable man. He droned on in a bitter monotone about the government whenever he watched the news or read the newspaper. This would continue when he took his pyjamas from the airing cupboard next to the fire and changed into them, his ribs protruding from his gaunt frame like barrel staves. May joined in with his peeves to some extent, as she had her fair share of bile too, but Jim was brimming with it.

Thirty years earlier, Jim had been engaged and his leaving home had been on the cards. He had been somewhat dashing then, cruising about town in his open top MG. His engagement had dragged on though, leaving his fiancée, Cora, tapping her fashionably-shoed foot. I had heard from my mother that when Cora would come over to Hilltop Road, her first port of call was the mirror above the fire-place where, chattering all the while about sundry frivolities, she would primp and preen her stylish hair and refresh her vermillion lipstick. 'She looks like she's been at the jam', May used to say. Jim had started building a bungalow on the land next to his mechanic's garage, with the idea that it would become the marital home but progress was slow, probably intentionally. His excuse of 'The house isn't finished yet' was his way of putting off the wedding.

After a number of years, sick and tired of waiting, Cora called it off, giving Jim back the ring, with its impressive emerald set in the middle of a rosette of diamonds. Soon after this, Jim discovered she was 'seein' anutha fella' and, carrying a hammer, went down to Whitehaven's main shopping street on a Saturday afternoon to find her. No words passed between them when he walked up to her. He simply dropped the ring at her feet, crouched down and hammered it into deformity before storming off. Cora, being a decent type, sent the ring, including the stones that had become unset, back to Hilltop Road, making sure it was delivered directly to May who hid it away.

Jim continued the slow tinkering with his bungalow for the next few decades, which was his justification for continuing to live at home. When it was approaching completion, he began using it as a store room, filling it with car parts and bits of steam engines, probably on purpose so that he'd have an excuse for never moving out. He was fascinated with steam power and built some cutting-edge contraptions that had once put him on the front of a now extinct periodical devoted to steam vehicles. In the cover shot, sporting a rare smile, he was afloat upon one of the great Cumbrian lakes in what looked like a steam-powered bathtub.

Jim had never been keen on his younger sister. His resentment had begun forty-five years earlier, the moment she'd been born. There was some excitement in the neighbourhood because May was in her forties so the pregnancy was certainly going to be her last and, after three boys, she had given birth to a girl! During World War II, when my mother was a small child and Jim in his twenties, he had been disgruntled if May ever gave her a share of the weekly chocolate ration because he wanted more for himself. Despite Jim's disagreeable nature, his father had worked hard to keep him out of the War when the possibility of conscription loomed, promptly engaging him as an electrician down the mine, an essential homeland occupation. As a survivor of the battlefields of World War I, Joseph decided that the mine was preferable to his son becoming a soldier. Always protective and acutely aware of the dangers of the mine, it had been Joseph who had set Jim up with an above ground electrician's apprenticeship when he left school and later had encouraged his younger sons to train as policemen. Perpetually ungrateful, Jim had once done something to infuriate the mild-mannered Joseph and my mother still remembered the scene. She had never seen her father so angry and, as a result of this, had been wary of Jim ever since.

Now, this loathed sister had returned to the family home which Jim regarded as his territory and, after a few weeks, he wasn't having it. He locked my mother out when she returned from work and, when she demanded to be let in, shouting 'Let me speak to my mother!', he came out and tried to shove her down the steps that led up to the front door. Inside the house, May was distressed but couldn't actively intervene: she felt too frail to risk a backlash from her volatile son. She had liked having her only daughter around for company and to help her with chores. All Jim did was bring home packets of meat, the blood soaking through the paper, which May would cook for their dinner. He never gave May any money towards the upkeep of the house as he said he didn't make enough from his mechanic's business. This was probably true as it was likely he was grumpy with customers. He was so temperamental that May had long since given up asking for any contribution from him. The time had come, therefore, for us to beat another hasty retreat so, the next day, we moved into a caravan on the seafront at St. Bees.

I'd always been enthusiastic about caravans. They are homes in miniature so it is understandable that children are drawn to them. A couple of our summer holidays as a family were to Rockley Sands Caravan Park in Dorset. Unfortunately, it was very far south and the drive was ghastly because I was prone to travel sickness. My mother dosed me up with a little blue tablet called Sea Legs, despite the journey being on dry land, but it never worked. I sat wedged between my older sisters who were dressed in the peculiar fashion of the day: flared trousers, tiered tops and platform shoes, which I prayed wouldn't be handed down to me. My sisters adorned themselves with pop music badges and other fan memorabilia, including a silky scarf that said 'Smile an Osmond Smile!'. It was decorated with five sets of large teeth which I thought resembled dentures. My sisters smelt of perfume and chewing gum and, to me, this was a nausea-inducing combination.

When we finally arrived at Rockley Sands, we collected the key for our allotted caravan. Holidays there were wonderful apart from the time my father dropped the metal-framed fold-down bed onto my forehead where I still have a scar, or when my mother fried spam and its stench would fill every fibreglass pore of the caravan. I'd go off to the beach unsupervised, where I'd do a lot of staring at the natural dioramas in rock pools. Every morning, I trudged over to the children's clubhouse, again unaccompanied, where for a couple of hours, cartoons shone onto a large pull-down screen from a rattling sixteen millimeter film projector, which I deemed superb entertainment. There was a lot of unaccompanied childhood activity in those days but the government's child safety information films— such as the terrifying one entitled, *The Spirit of Dark and Lonely Water*, featuring an anthropomorphic blanket with a cruel and hollow laugh who tempted foolish children to mess about at the edges of ponds filled with tangling weeds and littered with industrial rubbish—kept most of us on our toes.

Caravans in winter, however, are different kettles of fish, particularly when they're in the frigid north. Seagulls on the coast of West Cumbria are nearly the size of albatrosses and used the roofs of the caravans at St Bees as take off and landing strips, setting Jess the dog off barking at all hours. At Whitehaven harbour, these Cumbrian harpies would ambush anyone in possession of a bag of chips, swooping on them to grab the lot, not content to make do with the one or two spares tossed to placate them. I once saw one of their chicks struggling at the foot of a cliff and, when I went to see if I could help it, the powerful wing of the mother gull swiped my cheek as it screamed in my ear. Hurrying away, I noticed it had also bombed me from its nether end, necessitating an entire change of clothes. I resolved then and there that this would be the last time I'd ever try to do anything nice for a seagull.

St. Bees beach, one of the most beautiful beaches I'd ever seen, also happened to be buffeted most of the year by icy winds that made even Jess hurry back indoors. The single barred electric fire in the sitting room area was woefully inadequate so, after one shivering month, we were moving again.

My mother had arranged to rent a house on Loop Road, so called as it swooped right around the heights above Whitehaven. The house was neglected and had been empty for a few years but the garden was charming. There was a stream with a mossy bank and little stone bridges, an ornate wood-framed glass house with a rampant camelia and a strange stone monument at the back that I decided was a long forgotten gravestone.

Once we'd settled into the Loop Road house, my mother decided to re-enact the tradition of afternoon tea every Sunday in a room she set up like the old-fashioned parlour. She would drive May over and there would be other relatives for a gathering of the clan over dainty sandwiches, sponge cake and flapjacks. I wasn't in the best frame of mind to be sociable and used to feel particularly bothered by an older cousin who berated me for being quiet, with her oft-repeated question, 'Has the cat got your tongue?', for which I never had an answer. She'd laugh at my baggy clothes, describing my jumper as a 'bell tent' and telling me to stop being so 'droopy'.

I decided to play a trick on this cousin and emptied a jar of cod liver oil capsules into a small paper bag like the type they gave you in sweet shops. My mother had told me I needed to take one of these capsules every day to regain my lost pep but sometimes they would burst in my throat and the rotten fish taste made me retch. I held the paper bag out to this cousin and asked her if she wanted to try

one of these new sweets I'd discovered. With her
healthy appetite, she took one immediately and put
it in her mouth. I waited for the vile capsule to burst
and the reaction of dismay but my evil plan back-
fired when, to my surprise, she told me she found it
tasty and asked for another.

The Loop Road house was within walking distance
of Manda's but things had changed. I'd made a
comment regarding my father's extramarital affairs,
which I'd heard about from my mother, and it was
the only time Wiff ever became angry with me. I
didn't visit for a few weeks and then I heard he had
become ill.

Wiff had enjoyed a lifetime of rude health, which
was remarkable considering he'd been smoking
cigarettes since he was twelve. The first hint of
serious illness occurred when he attempted to fix the
ancient washing machine over which he had bent
and, in doing so, cracked a rib. Whilst he was
convalescing, bronchitis came on. Once he was
confined to his bed, I never again heard him whistle
his signature tune which had played about his lips
so often it was almost like a tic. Years later, I
chanced upon the '60s Greek film *Never on a
Sunday*, where the tune popped up as Melina
Mercouri's theme song in her role as an alluring
middle-aged courtesan in a silk kimono. She could
have been one of the pin-ups in Wiff's allotment shed
and I wondered whether his thoughts had been on
her as he whistled.

I brought him black grapes, of which he had
always been fond, but he couldn't swallow the skins
any longer so my mother held out a tissue for him to

spit them into. He was admitted to hospital and died in his sleep three days later.

The morning after his death, I was dropped off at Manda's. I was to have a couple of days off school to sit with her. When I arrived, she was alone by the gas fire, red-eyed and with a small embroidered handkerchief in her lap. I was inwardly distraught but could not cry, however hard I tried. A succession of people dropped in, each for around thirty minutes, and I spent the day making cups of tea in white porcelain cups, or 'china beakers' as she called them since they were a bit too dainty to call mugs. She had a couple of dozen of these china beakers because people always gave them to her as presents. They were invariably adorned with a spray of flowers, which branded them as an ideal gift for an old lady. As a former maid, she regarded it a great accomplishment to have tea in fine porcelain every day. On that day, her first as a widow, the phrase she said every time a new visitor arrived, which I heard even while I was busy with the kettle in the kitchen was, 'He was company for me, you know.'

There was a coffin maker two doors down from Manda's house. Whenever I walked past, I used to glance through the broken windows at the aptly named Mr. Casket, the stocky, bald proprietor, always busy making his coffins. He had to lean them up against the wall, one against the other, because he didn't have adequate space. But his was a steady trade and keeping up with the dead was a lucrative business. He made Wiff's coffin for a discount as they used to play dominos together in the pub.

My father came up to Whitehaven for the funeral,

bringing along a spare black suit for Eric, his older brother. Due to Eric being so much taller than my father—they had the nicknames 'big lad and 'little lad' growing up and it wasn't just about their age—the trousers were mid-calf length on Eric, which made even the grieving Manda laugh.

5

An Ideal Daughter

I saw Manda most days after Wiff died, preferring to go there rather than to school, not only because I wasn't going to get hurt, but also because it gave my life some purpose. Her words 'he was company for me' had struck a chord and I was ready to fill that empty chair, particularly if it involved homemade shortbread. So, on weekday mornings after my mother dropped me off near the school, I would wave goodbye and, as soon as the Mini Clubman had rounded the corner, would walk over to Manda's instead, usually taking a detour home to bring Jess along too. Richmond, with its sketchy register-taking, was not the kind of school to follow up on large numbers of absences. So I became, quite un-noticed, a school refuser for the next year. Manda, having left school at fourteen herself, only smiled when I told her that my school gave lots of time off and said nothing further about it.

I preferred the company of old people in those days and preferred to live the life of an old person, which even I, in my uneasy state of mind, thought was unusual for someone of my age. Manda was uncomplicated and cheerful, along with always being so pleased to see me. Adolescents need a routine and without the routine of school, I built mine around her. I would arrive, usually with Jess pulling me through the parlour hoping for short-bread, thus reminding me of one of her Mills and Boon titles, *Where The Wolf Leads*. I'd help her with 'little jobs', as she described them, things that were a bit much for someone of her age like cleaning the windows, whitewashing her yard wall, or assisting with the monthly task of polishing her numerous brass ornaments. 'I wish I'd had a daughter like you,' she would tell me. No one had ever said anything like that to me before.

We sat together with shortbread and tea, which I'd make to the correct hue of brown for her and she'd always declare 'Ah, that's a good cup of tea,' after the first sip. We'd watch one of her terrible daytime soap operas, *The Young Doctors*, from Australia, or the badly dubbed, and unintentionally comic melo-drama, *Zara the Slave Girl*, from Brazil. Manda had quite the international outlook for some-one who'd barely set foot outside of Whitehaven.

In the mornings, once or twice a week, we'd go up to the top of Main Street and visit her cousin, Sally Marshall, husky-voiced and chain-smoking, with an impossibly long cigarette ash which she always got to the ashtray in the nick of time. I never saw Sally without a hot water bottle on her lap, no doubt owing to her poor circulation from decades of smok-ing. On the wall above her television set was a large black and white framed photograph of her sister, Evelyn, who had 1940s movie star good looks, and was wearing a wartime volunteer's uniform.

Manda would bring Sally her pension and a few necessities from the corner shop. I'd make some tea, washing out the cups first because Sally couldn't get them very clean. When Sally became too ill to cope a few years later, she'd raged at the ambulance men to leave her be, so she could die in her own bed. They took her off to the hospital anyway, where she died still in high dudgeon at their presumption.

Back at Manda's, she would make lunch, usually meat and two veg with a simple dessert like tapioca, or 'frog spawn' as it was generally known, due to its slippery globules. She was grateful I was there to take a lunch tray over to her brother, known to everyone as Sen because, in his youth, he often sucked liquorice pellets called Sen-Sens.

Sen lived up a path across the meadow at the back of her house. I called him Uncle Sen and he always called me Audrey which, as I couldn't persuade him otherwise, I became resigned to. He insisted I take a mini Kit-Kat before departing. My childhood allergy for chocolate, amongst other things, had faded when I reached my teens and I was doing my best to catch up with everything I'd missed out on but, in spite of this, I could never bring myself to eat the Kit-Kat Sen offered me. Some of the foil had worn away and, because the chocolate bar was sitting in one of his dusty kitchen cupboards, I'd sneak it into a kitchen drawer before leaving. I now believe that the same Kit-Kat was perpetually making its way back up to the cupboard, where it was offered to me again the next time I brought Sen lunch.

Uncle Sen's house smelt feathery, like the racing pigeons he kept in a ramshackle wooden loft at the end of his garden. The hair on the top of his head stood up like soft, floaty down and he had round, dark, red-rimmed eyes, similar to his pigeons. He wore the mandatory Whitehaven old man's tweed cap, with matching carpet slippers, and his jumper was often accidentally threaded with a feather or two. I liked to look at the pigeons cooing through the chicken wire. They were startled at first but, if I was completely still, they grew accustomed to me and edged closer until, if I moved ever so slowly, I could stroke one of them with an extended finger.

Sen had been a widower for the last couple of decades. During the war, he and his wife had agreed to take part in a community scheme whereby piglets were billeted in various households where they would be fed on scraps. Eventually, the pigs were butchered to help alleviate the hardships of rationing. The problem was that Sen and his wife had been given a pig of an affectionate disposition who would sit between them when they rested on the grassy bank in their garden watching the sun go down, no doubt creating a most unusual silhouette. It was a sad day when the pig grew to the required size and the butchers came to collect her in the van. Stories like this nudged me further toward vegetarianism and it was at about this time that I started trying to subsist largely upon microwaved broccoli topped with melted cheddar cheese.

Early on in his dementia, I saw Sen from afar one day struggling to get his pigeons back into the loft after their exercise. Normally, they would come back as soon as their seed tin was rattled but, if that failed, he could always take out one of the white fantail doves and hold it up, flapping its wings, to attract them. On this occasion, it seemed that hadn't worked and he was shaking the white bird with anger. By the time I reached him, the dove was dead under a bush and he'd gone inside. Fortunately, the pigeons had by then started to return tentatively to the loft of their own accord and were arranging themselves on their perches. When they were all inside, I closed the loft doors and went down the garden path to his house to see if he was alright. He had dozed off in the armchair beside his gas fire. I noticed it still hadn't been repaired where he'd jabbed his poker into it a few months back, having forgotten he no longer had a coal fire.

Manda would occasionally go on coach tours exclusively for pensioners so that I wasn't able to tag along. When I saw her the day after a trip to Edinburgh, she shook her head in sorrow and said, 'I wish you'd been there, Petal'. After the long drive, the coach had disgorged the ill-fated pensioners next to a park on a busy thoroughfare. Manda, probably the most able-bodied of the lot, which included her cousin, Nelly Pape, who had dicey hips, could not fathom how to cross the dangerous main road to get her gang to the opposite side of the street where there were shops and cafes. After a few unsuccessful attempts, they gave up, spending the day on the benches next to where the bus had dropped them off and where it would collect them three hours later. All they could find for lunch on their side of the road was ice cream as there was a vendor at the entrance to the park. She regretted that she hadn't managed to bring me a box of the pastel-coloured, oddly chalky Edinburgh Rock and I reassured her that I didn't mind in the slightest.

Occasionally, I would dip back into Richmond School for a few days to perpetuate the illusion that I hadn't entirely disappeared, just in case one of the teachers cottoned on and phoned my mother. One of the rough girls in my year group, Dora, decided, surprisingly, to befriend me. Dora had a turban of mousy brown hair and lived on Mirehouse, which she pronounced 'Mirhus', one of the sprawling modern council estates that surrounded the town. She invited me over to a babysitting job at her next door neighbour's house with which she had, miraculously, been entrusted. I looked on with curious horror as she went through the drawers in the young couple's bedside cabinets and, using a fine needle, poked holes in their condom packs for a laugh. Sure enough, a few months later, the couple were expecting an unplanned baby they could scarcely afford.

Shortly after this incident, Dora urged me to sign up for the day trip to France led by that archvinophile, the loathsome French teacher, Mr. Ball. A bus would take us all the way from Cumbria to the ferry at Dover and, following the crossing, we would have a couple of unsupervised hours in Dunkirk, before driving all the way back again. Covering such a vast distance in one day should have put me off immediately, but I had fond memories of France that I was eager to rekindle: the clean air, the fresh bread, the beautiful landscapes. However, all that had been in the Loire Valley in summer, and we were going to Dunkirk, an industrial port town, in in winter. This trip ended up being one of the worst twenty-four hours of my life.

By the time we arrived, I was tired out. The bus emptied and Mr. Ball told us to be back on it in the same place, beside an ugly concrete *supermarche*, in two hours. We could do what we liked, he told us. I, of course, was fully prepared to ask for sanitary towels so that was one good thing.

Dora linked her arm through mine and steered me around Dunkirk, eyeing up the French boys. When one, posing on a run-down moped, eyed her back, I told her to be careful. She was not and the next moment they had become bawdy on his moped seat. I tried to disengage her from him but neither of them was having it and he drove his wheel into my leg to fend me off, while Dora laughed like a giddy schoolgirl on the verge of unhinged delirium. The bus was leaving in thirty minutes and I eventually persuaded her to come away, but not before he had torn her blouse and given her neck some ugly bites. As she begrudgingly walked back to the bus, she became more and more surly with me.

I wanted to buy Manda and my mother gifts but we passed no quaint shops, so I had to go into the concrete *supermarche* where the bus was parked. I stood in a line with some Belgian chocolate, whilst Dora had her arms full of cheap alcohol, a gift for herself. Behind us, an inebriated French tramp swayed, waiting to buy the largest bottle of cider I'd ever seen. Appropriately, he stank of rotten apples and urine and his odour made my cheeks redden and my head reel.

On boarding the bus, I noted that Mr. Ball had

piled two seats with a large number of cardboard boxes containing wine. The entire excursion must have been planned around his need to replenish his supply, courtesy of the school.

On the ferry on the way back, many of us had a few swigs of what Dora had bought, which was akin to rubbing alcohol. Dora didn't mind though and got herself hopelessly drunk. She 'snogged' any boy who'd have her, even Spewsy, who'd just had a bout of *mal de mer*. When I returned to my house on Loop Road, I fell asleep on the mat in front of the gas fire with the dog and didn't wake up for fifteen hours.

Dora had, upon our return, made the decision to despise me. The next time she saw me at school, I could barely understand the rapid-fire tirade with which she assailed me in her Cumbrian dialect. It seemed to have something to do with the moped interlude I had cut short, ruining her fine chance of being exotically deflowered on a vinyl seat held together with duct tape in full view of French pensioners sitting in cafes enjoying their croissants. The hormones were raging in that one so I ducked for cover and watched my back.

Dora breathed fire when any other girl went near me but Carol, one of the sensible girls, petite with golden hair and dazzling blue eyes, defied her and sat with me at lunch. Carol was later cornered at the bottom of the stairs and, through a throng of spectators, I watched Dora yank her head downward by her hair in order to repeatedly knee her in the face. The geography teaching Deputy Head waded in, ineffectually trying to stop her. Carol was driven to hospital with a bleeding nose and Dora sent to the headmaster. I expected Dora to be expelled but she was back two days later, laughing with her friends about the suspension she'd received. When Carol returned to school, she had a strange, new hardened attitude, along with sporting some quite severe make-up to hide her bruises. When these faded, she chose to keep wearing it. I was amazed to see Carol go over to the other side of the classroom a few days later, smile at Dora, and then start laughing at her crude jokes, no longer interested in being with me. Carol had forced a change in her nature in order to survive that I couldn't bring myself to make.

My attendance dropped off to nil after that. Cementing my wish to keep off school premises were frequent phone calls from Dora consisting of bombardments of expletives vividly describing how she was going to maim me. These calls made me feel sick and though I learned to put the phone down as soon as I heard her voice, I'd shake with anxiety. Yet, I never told anyone about it because I felt feeble and pathetic.

When I didn't go to Manda's, I spent the day at home on Loop Road in my nightdress, playing the migraine hand to my mother. In those troubled days, my dear dog, Jess, stepped into a Grace Poole role, whilst I was somewhat akin to the deranged Bertha Mason. Depressed and without any daily routine, I became more and more nocturnal and would go for walks around Whitehaven alone in the early hours to try to tire myself out, often strolling in the middle of the empty roads, surreally illuminated by the light from the orange street lamps. A car went past one time and everyone inside stared at me. When I was finally able to drop off in bed, I would sometimes sleepwalk, waking up in odd places, such as the time I found myself outside on the pavement in my nightdress, staring down the street.

Unbeknown to us, Jim, who'd told my mother about the Loop Road house when it came up for rent, had a front door key. I was there alone on the occasion that he was asked to do some maintenance work for the owner who was an acquaintance of his. When I was alone at home, I would bolt the door to feel extra safe. One day, I heard a persistent knocking, which was strange because no one ever came to the house on weekdays so I decided not to answer it. The knocking then turned into furious pounding that went on for some time. When I finally plucked up the courage to peep through the curtain, I was shocked to see Jim's enraged face looking back at me, 'Yer little bugger, open't bloody door!' he shouted. I quickly unbolted it and then dashed upstairs, in case he dashed me, and locked myself in the bathroom. Of course, I probably should never have let him in but I wasn't a strong-minded teenager.

Quite soon after that, my mother began to look for a house to buy. She'd needed to finalise her divorce with my father so that the court would compel him to release the funds from her portion of the house in Wales. He came up to Cumbria and the three of us, smartly dressed, went to visit someone legal, a family court judge perhaps, whose half-moon glasses struck me as peculiar as I'd only ever seen the like of them in Dickens adaptations on television. We all sat around a long polished table and the legal man read things out that I couldn't follow and then asked me if I wanted to live with my mother. It reminded me of the time just before we left Caerleon when I was asked whether I liked my father. The same feeling of not knowing what to say left me silent. I didn't want to single one of them out in front of the other. However, my father, sitting opposite, nodded encouragingly so I quietly replied to the legal man in the affirmative.

My mother bought a house in Moresby Parks, a windswept old mining settlement a few miles outside Whitehaven which consisted of two rows of terraces, the original housing for the miners and their families, along with a newer estate of council houses with gardens, hence the 'Parks' addition. The pit was now closed. A couple of miles away was the very different Low Moresby, a quaint little hamlet near a mini proscenium arch theatre, Rosehill. My friend, Rachel from Richmond, lived there in a beautifully converted stone barn and I visited occasionally. Compared to Low Moresby, Moresby Parks was stark and grey.

Our house was on the end of a terrace where local adolescents amassed, leaning on our window sills and sitting on our step, probably because they had been ordered to 'Go play out, yer mithering us to death!' by indifferent parents. You could even see pairs of eyes watching our television through the cracks in our Venetian blinds. There was also the aggravation of being the handiest door to play knock and run away, which was the apogee of excitement for them.

My mother grew tired of their antics and of the gale force winds whipping through the outcrop where our house was situated. She sold up within a year and we moved to an uninspiring but convenient modern red brick flat in Whitehaven on the pleasantly named High Meadows estate, but with any trace of its pastoral past long since obliterated.

Unlike me, my mother had become fully settled in the land of her forefathers. She had joined the Ramblers' Club and there proved herself an expert map reader, going out for the day to do 'recces' in preparation for leading the other hill walkers the following week. I went on some outings with the club from time to time, but, ill-nourished, unfit and sleep deprived as I was, found it hard to keep up with the seasoned ramblers, most of whom were decades older than me.

Through the rambling club, my mother had made a lot of new friends. She became particularly friendly with Roger, whose wife joined the walks only occasionally. Roger, who was an insurance salesman, had grown up children and a problematic marriage. I had been on one of the walks when his wife was present but didn't cotton on to this. My mother took a shine to Roger, often being the only one to laugh at his obscure jokes or the droll raising of one of his eyebrows. He started popping round to our flat after work for a meal and had some unusual requirements when he ate, such as asking for a glass of milk whenever he was served chips as this would 'cut the grease'. My mother pandered to his whims, probably because she had waited so many years for the tingle of love to return to her. On a few occasions, I overheard him claim that he resembled an older Errol Flynn which I couldn't really see. However, he did have one famous connection in that he was a distant cousin of a well known Cumbrian poet. There was an LP in Whitehaven Library, which I'd borrowed a few times, featuring this poet reading his work. I had some favourite lines that I hoped Roger might be familiar with, but he wasn't and they didn't interest him. Although Roger had a passing physical likeness to his distant relative, he showed no fondness for any kind of poetry.

Evening meals progressed into occasional all-nighters and, after a month or so of this, the phone rang at 2 am. Not being a good sleeper, I dashed into the sitting room to answer it. It was Roger's grown up son telling me he knew his father was there with my mother and that he needed to go to the hospital because his mother had harmed herself in reaction to his infidelity. I was shocked by this and knocked on my mother's bedroom door, telling them through the keyhole, what had happened. My mother didn't thank me and was quite miffed that I had answered the phone. Roger left for the hospital and over the next few days arrangements were swiftly made for his wife to move to Yorkshire to live with her son and his family. Once things had settled down, Roger resumed his relationship with my mother.

One day, following his evening meal, Roger confided to my mother that he didn't think I liked him as I seldom smiled when he arrived. It was true, I was rarely chipper and how ever hard I tried, I couldn't find my way out of the gloom. He often saw me engrossed in one of the generally bleak, black and white old movies I was drawn to at that time. My favourites, among them, D.W. Griffith's *Orphans of the Storm* and G.W. Pabst's *Diary of a Lost Girl*, both had tragic young female leads. Films like these, with stories about young ladies who were a lot worse off than I was, but for whom things came out alright in the end, served to give me hope.

On a routine check up at the veterinary clinic with Jess, I asked our Scottish veterinarian if he could offer me some work experience. I thought I might give myself a structure by focusing on a possible career to aim for. I knew that the highly scientific university course to become a vet was out of the reach of a school refuser but, with my fondness for animals, I was toying with the idea that I could be able to be a veterinary assistant one day. The vet was a nice fellow who'd given me a free hamster with unusual black and white markings the year before, hence my naming the rodent Humbug. He said I could help him in his surgery one evening per week, as well as accompanying him on some of his farm visits.

The surgery was on the ground floor of a tall terraced house a short walk from the town centre. I proved myself quick to learn the names of different pieces of equipment and was able to pass them to the vet when he asked for them. He always explained what he was doing and I soon got to know the names of all the parasites that plague a dog's life. Once the vet was out on an urgent call and his surgery was going to open late. The junior partner had been phoned and was on his way. The vet's wife, whom I'd never seen before, beckoned me upstairs to wait. She looked a good ten years younger than her husband and had short dark hair and a pleasant, if mischievous, face. She offered me a glass from the bottle of wine she was drinking, which I declined. 'What do you think of my husband's junior partner?' she slurred, 'He's quite attractive, don't you find? I think he's absolutely captivating.' At this point the junior partner appeared at the door to collect the surgery keys. 'Och, we were just saying how gorgeous you were!' I was mortified by this but the junior partner, seemingly accustomed to such antics, took the keys and retreated.

One evening, the vet rang me and asked if I wanted to accompany him on a call to a farm in the countryside. He collected me and we drove over there. On the way, he tutted about the farmer, whose habits he was familiar with, and whom he suspected had probably left things to the last minute because he didn't want to pay. Arriving at the farm, which was in a sorry state, the farmer, attired in the standard Cumbrian older man garb of flat cap and trenchcoat, greeted us with an appropriately sheepish smile. The pregnant ewe at his feet was on her side, panting and her lamb was stuck in the birth canal. We rolled the sheep over onto her back and propped her end up on a hay bale. The vet then filled her up with soap flakes and delved in. Twin lambs, probably dead, was his prognosis. Putting his hands inside her again, he tied cords to the lambs' legs and together we pulled each one out. Both were perfectly formed but both dead, as predicted. The farmer had waited so long that the mother was possibly going to die too, the vet said. We drove back and, soon after, I gave up on veterinary assistant as a job I might one day be able to do.

I'd been in Cumbria for nearly two years and things had gone from sad to sadder for me. Life had stood still. I'd not made any progress and had whiled away the hours in a daze. I'd lived in four different houses and had barely been to school. Of course, I always had Manda to comfort me but I didn't reveal my inner gloom to her. In fact, I made her laugh most of the time. So, just before my sixteenth birthday, I decided to return to the last place where things had gone well for me, at least with regard to school. To my mother's surprise, I announced that I wished to go back to live with my father in Wales. It was supposed to be for the next two years; it would last for four months.

6

Beware Attempts to Recapture the Past

Jess the dog, Humbug the hamster and me, Misery the teenager, were dropped off back in Caerleon in the August that I turned sixteen. My mother exhibited a mixture of relief, as I was a morose old thing, and trepidation as my father wasn't really concerned with basic human needs when it came to anyone other than himself. The first thing I noticed was the griminess of the house and the lack of food other than a half-eaten block of Cracker Barrel cheddar in the fridge. It hadn't been sealed up properly so the cheese was dry and cracked around the edges. I should have expected this as my mother had done the shopping while they were married along with being the maid of all work. The cleaning could wait, however, because I was ready to seek out my old friends whom I'd been corresponding with since I'd left. Naturally, I made a beeline for Andrea's house.

During our early secondary school years, when we were segregated into 'clevers' and 'averages', Andrea had introduced my average mind to Shakespeare because he was only on the clevers' curriculum. I'd urged her to tell me every detail of every scene of the

Zeferelli film of *Romeo and Juliet* which they'd watched in class. She had a school paperback of the play with the cover falling off and we read it together in her house, enough times that the cover did eventually fall off. Over the two years that followed, by way of Andrea, I also discovered *Macbeth* and *A Midsummer Night's Dream*.

We had been an enterprising pair. The second summer I'd been there, we were bored during the holidays and no longer wished to relive our former entertainments of wandering about the grounds of the mental hospital, hanging around in church services and sitting on the village green eating buns. Instead, we resolved to organise a fete on our road to raise money for the charity, Guide Dogs for the Blind. No one gave us this idea, we just got on with it, despite our youth and inexperience, using the archetypal village fete as our model, albeit on a smaller scale that would fit into the end of our cul-de-sac. We had a cake stall, a guess the number of sweets in the jar competition, a plant stall, a bric-a-brac stall, a tombola and a raffle with a giant teddy bear as first prize, all on borrowed tables.

In preparation for these fetes, of which we held two in consecutive summers, we set up what could be termed a junior marketing and advertising agency, enlisting other kids to come round and draw posters. These kids would then be sent out to put their posters up on lampposts and hand them to owners of little shops around the estate.

We'd trawl around the neighbourhood, knocking on doors, selling raffle tickets, receiving donations of prizes or things to sell and exhorting everyone to come along. Most people were impressed that some kids were helping a charity off their own bat. There was one fellow on our road, however, whom we called The Werewolf on account of his unkempt beard, who'd always shut the door in our faces with a 'Not today, thank you!' so we'd return the next day. On the day of the fete, I put a large tartan bow on my dog's collar and dozens of people attended. We raised hundreds of pounds, receiving badges and car stickers from the Guide Dogs Association in thanks.

When bonfire night was on the horizon, we applied the same model for two consecutive bonfire nights for an event that took place in the field at the end of our road. In a wheelbarrow, we made the rounds with the elaborate, life-size guy I'd created but we didn't stoop to saying 'Penny for the Guy', choosing instead a more refined approach to raising money for fireworks by selling 'bonfire night tickets'. Each hand-made ticket entitled the bearer to a foil-wrapped potato, baked in the coals of the bonfire, a piece of homemade parkin and attendance at a firework display which would be safely managed by my responsible neighbour who was, I liked to inform people, a biology teacher. It was fun to return to the house of The Werewolf in an attempt to sell him a ticket and receive another, 'Not today, thank you!'

By the time I returned from Whitehaven, however, Andrea had already left school and started at the secretarial college in the nearby industrial city of Newport. She went there on the bus every weekday in a pencil skirt, nylon tights, white blouse, wool blend coat, make-up and hair puffed into a 1980s bouffant with blonde highlights. She wouldn't hear of it when I begged her to come back to school in with me September, where we could study Shakespeare in the same class as there was no segregation in the sixth form. She said she never wanted to set foot in a school again.

My mother had also gone to her local typing and shorthand college at the age of sixteen, right after school. It was an expected route for a tidy, working class girl who was good with figures, spelling and grammar when the university track was not yet an option that was normally considered. Andrea was the only child of doting, older parents and they'd gladly have supported something more ambitious than this humdrum progression, but their daughter simply wasn't interested and I could see for myself that the spark had gone out of her eyes.

My father had earmarked me from an early age for this same secretarial college in Newport. As soon as I had been assigned to the average stream, he decided that this would be an appropriate career for me. Also, with my strong skills in art, he thought I'd have no problem learning shorthand. He had concluded, even before I went to Whitehaven, that I'd immediately be able to get a job with a reasonable living wage and, if I played my cards right, be firmly established in the middle classes by using what appeared to be emergent good looks to marry the boss. A young lady with naturally long eyelashes and shapely calves that would look good in nylon tights could, thereby, have ideal prospects.

Now that I was back under his roof, he did not agree at all with my new plan to return to the comprehensive school to do the exams I'd not turned

Richmond before progressing to A-levels and, thereafter, perhaps, to university. He urged me to reconsider his original plans for me. It occurred to me during one of these discussions that when my father spoke to me and other relations, he used his mild Cumbrian accent, but with other people, even the neighbours, he used a pseudo-posh managing director's accent. The vowels were all muddled up though so that 'just' became 'jast' and 'black' became 'bleck'. Another strange thing he would do was, chameleon-like, to adopt the accent of whomever he was speaking to. So, chatting with an American acquaintance from the golf club on the phone, he slipped into Americanisms like 'sure thing' and 'God damn it!'. He appeared to be confused about his identity.

Meanwhile, what baffled me most about Andrea was that, having recently turned sixteen, she was sexually active, and had been for over a year, generally on the back seat of her boyfriend's car. It all seemed a bit on the sleazy side. They would go to empty car parks at night, often with Andrea's petite friend, Gemma, and her boyfriend who would park opposite in his car. Gemma had hardly grown since she was eleven and was now going to the same secretarial college, dressed in a similar secretarial uniform, looking like a little girl playing dress-up in her mother's clothes.

Andrea's boyfriend, the son of a prolific pig farmer, was an amiable eighteen-year-old. He put up with my sarcastic humour, which was a veil to cover my disappointment that he'd stolen away my former best friend. Once, while he was changing from tractor jeans to going out jeans at Andrea's, I'd snatched the good jeans off him and ran down the street with them, whilst he pursued me in his underpants. I then climbed up a lampost and tied them to the top. Fortunately, he found it all a good laugh. Thinking back though, I can see that I was puerile and irritating. Andrea married him a couple of years later, looking tiny in a lacy, tiered dress that rivaled her showpiece wedding cake. He built a modern house for them on the farm and in their sitting room hung a large canvas-effect photo of the two of them at their wedding. I only visited once because we fell out about the way the pigs were kept, droves of them corralled in pens, shot full of chemicals and in total darkness, the standard intensive farming regimen.

Returning to the comprehensive, I was something of a talking point and was warmly welcomed back. Most of the people who'd stayed on for sixth form were from Andrea's clever sphere. Almost no one from the lower clusters remained, all of them having signed up for vocational courses at colleges or gone straight into unskilled jobs. Since my departure, I'd blossomed in a certain regard about which I was quite self-conscious, but which prompted numerous boys to race each other to ask me out on a date. Psychologically, I was not at all ready for this, despite the physiological evidence to the contrary, but I told them all I was happy to go on a stroll or have a game of frisbee.

On the first 'date' I accepted, the poor chap appeared at the edge of the village green dressed up to the nines in a jacket and tie which, he confided, his mother and grandmother had helped him pick out. This immediately gave me an ominous feeling as, to my mind, we were off on nothing more than a stroll and I'd even brought the dog. He insisted that I walk on the inside of the pavement, which was peculiar and only served to annoy me by placing me in the role of a vulnerable female in need of protection. When he eventually leaned in for an embrace, I had to be quick-witted and piped up with 'Would you like to walk in the graveyard to read the old inscriptions?'.

'No, why would you want to go there and do that?' he replied, with the expected degree of astonishment somehow enhanced by his Welsh accent.

'Aren't you familiar with 'Pleasing Melancholy or A Walk among the Tombs in a Country Churchyard?"

'I've never heard of it.'

'Haven't you read *A Young Lady's Miscellany*?'

'Not that I can remember.'

I trotted him over there anyway. He fiddled with his tie and buttoned up his jacket against the dampening dusk. I showed him around the fine carvings of angels and the fancy scripts on the Victorian and Georgian gravestones, pointing out old yew trees here and there and wondering aloud about the lives these dead had once led. As he tapped the mulch from his shiny shoes, I could see the lust dropping away from his face. The next day, once he'd gossiped about it to his chums and the anticipated reaction was realised: no more date requests. I loved old graveyards and was, therefore, in their imaginations, a ghoulish girl, which suited me perfectly.

The ideal next step to this story would have been that I knuckled down, caught up with the work I'd missed and went off to university two years later but, alas, it was not to be. Try as I might, I was unable to concentrate on anything, probably due to the experiences of the past two years. I had jiggling knee syndrome and couldn't sit still to take in so much as a chapter of one of the books I was supposed to be reading. I'd had a vague hope before my return to Wales, that my father would make an effort to help me out of my quagmire but he wasn't interested. Much of the time he was out of the house, staying with Barbara, a middle-aged woman who worked on the production line at the factory in Newport where he was the director. Soon after I arrived, he announced their upcoming nuptials.

It surprised me that someone was interested in my father even with his generous salary. Perhaps he'd thus far hidden the less attractive aspects of his character but, all the same, he wasn't exactly pleasing to the eye either. He'd been a cute child and a boyishly handsome teenager but his face had been, quite literally, harvested by quack doctors in the 1950s. He had broken his nose playing rugby and, instead of repairing the septum, it had simply been removed and discarded. This meant that, as he aged, there was no support for his face and he looked like he was melting. Then there were his teeth, or lack of them. A dentist had claimed that, as a result of my father having unusually white teeth, they must therefore be as weak as chalk and had taken them all out. The treatment and the new set of false teeth had set back the gullible Manda a small fortune.

Whenever my father returned home from Barbara's house, I generally needed money with which to purchase some basic sustenance or school supplies. This infuriated him to such an extreme that, after a few weeks of my requests, he screwed up a five pound note and flicked it into my face. It was at that point I decided that I needed a Saturday job but the only one I was offered was at Benny's, a greasy spoon in Newport, to which I travelled by bus.

Under the more rigorous health and safety regimen of the present day, Benny's would probably be closed down. It was a couple of bus stops before the town centre and was the archetypal shabby all day breakfast joint with fixed formica tables and padded vinyl benches with missing buttons. The glass cabinet displaying the food was piled with sausages, fried bread and scrambled egg, all of which would be revitalised under the grill for the customer's delight. Many cups of tea were ordered there and I was instructed to reuse tea bags until the beverage came out almost clear.

Benny himself was a haggard-looking fellow with a thinning pate of shoulder-length ringlet curls. He sat at one of the cafe tables watching over us with large pale eyes. Occasionally, if you were doing something such as reheating a sausage in what he considered to be the incorrect way, he'd come forward and demonstrate, imparting the knowledge of one who'd been in the catering industry for decades. Wages were rock bottom but, to me, enough for basic necessities. Benny had a kind side though, giving free meals to a destitute old man who used to come in and shout out words of wisdom such as, 'Money is the God!', which I wholeheartedly agreed with at the time. Thin tea was also proffered generously. The job was hard on my legs with its ten hour shifts but it kept me going for a couple of months.

A few weeks into my experiment of living with my father, I began to take after him by going on drinking binges. I don't know why I indulged in this as I'd always been horrified by my father's example in that respect. He'd been a functioning alcoholic since his thirties. I could remember cringing with embarrassment as a girl when my mother returned from a jaunt to Spain with him and told me about his antics at Madrid airport. He had passed out in departures and other tourists had had no option but to step over him as he was splayed across a thoroughfare. My mother had sat at a distance, hoping that no one would associate her with him. Now I was guzzling booze like he did. It started off in the quaint village pubs around Caerleon, where boys would buy me drinks so they could sit with me and give me the occasional hug. This gradually descended into gatherings in freezing cold council flats dotted with seamy teenage couples canoodling in corners. I'd generally stand in the kitchen with a gaggle of alcoholic young people, rattling on about nothing I could remember the next day.

Another time, I went to a more upmarket party in a hotel ballroom with Andrea, having arranged to stay over in her spare room. There were cocktails at this event, which were something I'd never had before. To me, they tasted sweet and fruity so I downed a number in rapid succession before collapsing. Some friends of Andrea's offered to drop me off at her house on their way home. They carried me in, deposited me on the bed in the spare room and left. They hadn't realised that the electric blanket was on and I awoke the next morning, encrusted in my own warm vomit that had been baking nicely through the night. I felt lucky to have survived this since I could easily have choked or been electrocuted in my oblivious state. Andrea's good-natured parents ran a bath for me, gave me breakfast and insisted that I lie down on the couch while they changed the bed. At this point, I decided to moderate my drinking and possibly even give up alcohol altogether.

My father's intended, Barbara, moved in and re-decorated the house in her garish taste, papering over any trace of my mother who was not to be men-tioned in her presence. If she accidentally slipped into the conversation, my father would hurriedly refer to her as 'The Duchess' and they would smirk together. Barbara's bizarre son, who was my age, also moved in and promptly painted his new bedroom entirely black, even the ceiling. I tried to keep out of the house as much as possible because my new 'stepbrother' would attempt to molest me whenever his mother and my father were out at work. If he had a friend round, I'd generally have to fend off the two of them.

It was at about this time that I had my first go at having a boyfriend, mainly because I thought it would deter the stepbrother. This boyfriend was a few years older than me and in some kind of apprentice office job. He looked like the young Paul McCartney, whom I'd always found quite nice in the early Beatles films so I agreed to 'go out' with him. He was decorous enough that he called round at my house and asked my father's permission to take me out to the cinema in Newport on our first date. It was all very respectable, marked by old-time charm which made me feel that I wouldn't be subject to any rampant behaviour. Unbeknownst to me, however, my new boyfriend had a more demure identical twin brother. It was not until after a couple of weeks that they revealed I'd sometimes been on the phone with the brother, and had also been out with him on a couple of dates. Fortunately, this sharing of my charms had all been quite sedate, kisses and cuddles at the most. The relationship ended with a joyless attempt to consummate it, which took place in their parents' council house at midnight on the kitchen floor. I decided, in the nick of time that I just couldn't go through with it, and gentleman that he (Or perhaps his twin?) was, this was fine with him (Or should I say them?). He (or his brother), graciously walked me home and I never called him, or rather them, again.

It had escaped my notice, meanwhile, that Barbara was starting to resent me for reasons I didn't understand. Admittedly, neither of us had gone out of our way to befriend the other. I'd stayed out or up in my room most of the time she was in the house. This culminated in a disagreeable incident during Sunday lunch in a pub in a nearby village. The dessert menu had been perused and Barbara had followed her son's lead in opting for Black Forest gateau. My father had mock-scolded her as she was a plump lady and she had stormed off and remained absent for twenty minutes while we three ate our mediocre desserts in silence. After looking for her, we'd got into the car and started driving home. She soon came into view, stomping along by the side of the highway. My father pulled over and sarcastically asked her if she needed a lift. Her haughty response was 'Not with that cew in the car'. 'Cew' was her Welsh pronunciation of cow and she was referring to me, much to my surprise, as it wasn't me who'd mock-scolded her with the allusion to her weight. I was then ejected from the car by my father, who wanted to get off the hook and to put me on it in his place, while she was driven home. When I finally got to the house an hour or so later, my father was sitting in the car in the drive as he had, in his turn, been ejected from the house. On seeing me, he darted out and shoved me at the top of the steep flight of steps that led to the front door. I grabbed the handrail just in time to prevent a tumble. Without a word, I retreated to my room in a state of numb misery.

Barbara and my father made up and were soon married at the local registry office, followed by a meal in a posh hotel for about seventy people, before whom he lavished upon her a fox fur stole and a gold watch. She had gained the ultimate prize and married the boss but I wondered how long it would last.

The Sunday after their wedding, at the request of Barbara's parents, we all drove to a small Welsh Valleys church where they had been married fifty years previously. They had asked the Reverend to 'bless' their daughter's new marriage from his pulpit following his sermon. The narrow hedge-lined roads were irritating to my father in his bulky managing-director's car. When he tried to park by the church, he blew up at a van coming towards him that didn't give him enough room. He reddened with rage and waved his fist out of the window, as he often did when he felt challenged on the roads. Inside the church, when the service was due to begin, I found it quite amusing when the driver of the van appeared in the pulpit in his Reverend apparel. He did not bless their wedding after his sermon.

The two of them duly went off on a ten-day honeymoon, whilst the stepbrother was dropped off at his grandparents. Perhaps they'd secretly known all along that he was a molester who couldn't be left alone with me overnight. What I planned to do next was enact the typical 'troubled teen home alone' cliché: I held a party.

Up to this point, I'd only experienced one gate-crasher in my life. Jeremy was wan but with vivid hair the colour of undiluted orange squash, and he had turned up, uninvited, at my older sister's eighteenth birthday party. He thanked his generous hosts by drinking too much and vomiting on the carpet. This should have served as a warning regarding the gatecrasher's typical lack of gratitude.

I learnt that night that there was another key attribute to teen house parties, namely the expectation that attendees felt they must get down to a bit of hanky-panky in some shape or form in a semi-public location. Part of the thrill of this seemed to be finding the place to do it, be it behind a couch, in the cupboard under the stairs, or perhaps even in a child's bedroom while they were asleep, which was, unfortunately, how my sister's eighteenth birthday party ended for me. Perhaps an hour after I'd been told to go up to my room and get to sleep, I'd become aware of a couple sitting on the floor at the end of my bed. I was first alerted to their presence when the girl asked the boy, in an Irish accent, 'Are you sure that kid's asleep?' He replied in the affirmative and carried on with kissing her. I did not know what to do so I pretended to be asleep and tried to block out the irritating sound of their smacking lips. Finally, deciding enough was enough, I moved about as if I was stirring in my sleep which made them quietly leave as they thought I was waking up.

Now here I was, throwing my very own wild party. I'd been on the liberal side with invitations, extending them to people I barely knew, and amiably agreeing that they could 'bring along a couple of mates'. I later heard that everyone on the packed 9 pm double decker bus that stopped at the end of my road got out there. Someone had joked that the bus should've had my address set as the destination on the front.

When the house was filled well beyond capacity, people spilled into the garden. As they drank more and more, the police were called by the neighbours and, in my tipsy state, I quite rudely told them I had everything under complete control and that they should go away. Following a few outbreaks of violence, seemingly over who was going to have sex with whom, a few energetic spells of vomiting and some windows and shelves smashed, the house gradually began to empty out. By 3 am, I helped the remaining handful of laggards to find places to sleep.

I gave my bed to Haydn, a handsome blonde boy whom I was quite fond of. He chivalrously said I could sleep with him if I liked, but feeling I couldn't add any further complications to my perturbed life, I declined. I slept under a towel in the bathtub, which was remarkably uncomfortable and cold, like reposing in a round-cornered metal coffin, an apt metaphor for my state of mind at the time.

The next day, a few benevolent remainers hung around and helped me clean up the bomb site. Andrea enlisted her father, dressed in his dark blue mechanic's overalls, to come over and be a handyman. The trouble was, my father and Barbara were due to return that evening so there was insufficient time in which to get everything back in order. Of course, it's totally clear to me now, as it was partly even then, that I'd done this 'accidentally on purpose' since it would be sure to prove the final nail in my coffin. The trouble was, I had no Plan B.

They returned and were told what had happened out on the street by Andrea's father who wanted to prepare them for the worst. The house was clean enough but there were still a couple of broken windows, which he hadn't been able to fix because they needed special glass. Barbara sauntered in in her fox fur and called me 'a little whore'. This was quite a development from a 'cew', and was, frankly, a tad hyperbolic addressed to a peculiarly prudish girl who had an aversion even to French kissing.

A couple of days after this, Jess the dog and I—Humbug, the hamster, having expired during my brief Welsh sojourn—were forthwith returned to Whitehaven. My father drove me as far as a desolate service station in the vicinity of Wigan, where I was handed over to my mother who would take me the rest of the way. It hadn't come as a surprise to my mother that things with my father had fallen apart and, fortunately, she accepted me back without hesitation.

In Whitehaven, I promptly developed glandular fever and spent my first two weeks back in my mother's flat in bed, more ill than I could recall ever having been before. The main thing was, I felt safe because my mother knew and tolerated my foibles, whereas my father was rattled by them, and his new wife and stepson only saw me as either something to compete with or a groping opportunity. Three months later, my father and Barbara separated, and were divorced within a year of marrying. Manda told me that my father had claimed it was 'because of the way she treated you' but I was more inclined to believe it was about two selfish individuals, each of whom had soon realised that they were not going to get what they were after from the other, namely high status and a bountiful expense account for her and a cleaner, cook and default bedroom partner for him.

7

Wending one's Way to Womanhood

In the absence of any ideas, I decided to follow Rachel, my friend from Richmond, to Wyndham School in the nearby town of Egremont, a town famed for only one thing, the gurning world championship, which takes place at the annual Crab Apple Fair. The winner of said championship is he or she who can pull the ugliest face, usually aided by the removal of false teeth. This monstrous visage is then, for reasons lost to history, inserted through a horse collar. The last time Queen Elizabeth visited West Cumbria, the welcoming committee had the recent winner greet her and he duly performed his gurn framed by the horse collar. She did not look amused.

Rachel and I were hoping to scrape together enough qualifications to progress to the next stage of life. She had a plan to go on a hairdressing course in a few months' time, whereas I had no clue about my next step other than probably doing some A-levels to prolong my school experience and delay any career decisions.

I went to the school with my mother to sign up. The modern sixth form building was clad in wood that had seen better days and looked as if it had been scorched, I hoped not by some disgruntled student. The Head of Sixth Form asked me what I wanted to do after school and I shrugged despondently. My mother was exasperated because I hardly spoke but I felt abashed by the Head's intense blue eyes as he tried to fathom what to do with the impassive youth before him.

When I started at Wyndham, I was relieved to hear that most of the students were not afflicted with the incomprehensible accent that had baffled me at Richmond. They spoke a milder and slower version which I could follow. I found a safe niche in tiny catch up classes with kindly teachers. I had to acquaint myself with a whole new history curriculum as the socialist history teacher preferred the Jarrow Crusade and the Corn Laws to the Third Reich and the Treaty of Versailles. I needed to study a science subject so I took the easiest one on offer, environmental science. Mr Ray, the botanically minded teacher, often took us out on field trips to the moors where he inspired us with his love of sphagnum moss and wild cranberries. He arranged a visit to an iron ore pit and we came out rust-coloured. He even signed us up for an outward bound expedition that involved climbing up an underground waterfall. For me, in these first few months at Wyndham, he was a vital person in every sense and, for the first time in nearly three years, I began to feel settled in a school.

There was no uniform in the sixth form but I dressed in one all the same: an inconspicuous suit of jeans and a denim jacket that I always kept firmly buttoned. The sixth form common room was nerve-racking for me because it was in the form of a wide catwalk with roughly sawn wooden benches on either side, covered in worn out foam pads in brown covers. Classrooms were at both ends and walking down this catwalk to get to certain classes was hard because I had the misguided idea that everyone's eyes were upon me. I soon saw a way around this by going outside and entering through the doors at the other end. Stewart, a confident boy, whom I soon learned generally got the main parts in school plays, liked to walk from one end of the common room to the other in assured slow motion, seemingly in the hope that his arms, built up by much lifting of weights, were being fully appreciated in his pressed A-shirts.

There was another male who exhibited himself in that room but, so it seemed, not from vanity so much as from a genuine love of performing. The first thing that struck me about Ferg was his wavy shoulder-length brown hair partially tamed by an elasticated olive green headband. I then had a proper look at the rest of him: flared jeans, faded cheesecloth shirt and a fringed canvas shoulder bag. These things had gone out of fashion over ten years ago but he didn't care. In the common room, he would put on cassette tapes of curious tracks he'd recorded from the late night radio sessions of the alternative D.J., John Peel. Ferg devised a movement routine to accompany one of these mysterious wonders entitled 'Let's Evolve!' by Sudden Sway, an obscure pop group, in which, with some keen apprentices, they would start off as wriggling amoebas and gradually work their way up into more complex life forms. Ferg was a radiant being and, of course, I was too afraid to speak to him.

I gravitated towards Gill and Jill, or 'the two G/Jills' as they were generally known. They were inseparable and, like me, were encased entirely in denim. We were in the same catch up classes so we took to going about together. Another new friend, the ever cheerful Matthew, liked to keep a baked potato in the pocket of his black wool donkey jacket. He'd buy one at breaktime from the canteen and in his pocket it would remain, keeping him warm until he was ready to eat it. I visited him once at his home, a Victorian villa, where his parents ran a guest house for contractors from the nearby nuclear power station. With the rest of the house otherwise occupied, Matthew and his siblings were relegated to the dim basement with thin partition walls between each of their individual living spaces but they were a good-humoured troupe who got on well together. The two G/Jills press-ganged Matthew, who was perhaps even more shy than I was, into sending me an anonymous Valentine's card, over which matter I chided them for being presumptuous matchmakers.

Although I was no longer a school refuser, I still visited Manda regularly with Jess. We'd walk over through Beck Bottom, a park which used to have a row of houses in front of the beck, or brook, that had eventually been demolished due to frequent flooding. It was in one of these houses that Manda and Wiff had raised their two sons. When I arrived with Jess, Manda would rub my cold hands saying, 'Oh, you're starved!' and I often was, albeit in a more conventional sense, as my mother remained a convinced carnivore barely accommodating my newfangled vegetarianism in her cooking or shopping. So, as in days of yore, I'd raid the biscuit tins in the cupboard under the stairs.

At about this time, my eldest sister became aware of my amateurish approach to vegetarianism, which was heavily laden with sugary snacks, and sent me *The Cranks Recipe Book*. I began to follow the recipes, often with excellent results. My old cookery teacher, Mrs. Shackleton would have been proud. My 'signature dish' became Tarragon Eggs En Cocotte, which was relatively simple despite its fancy French name; it was just eggs baked in spoonfuls of cream on a bed of chopped tomatoes with sauteed onions and the vaunted tarragon. At Wyndham, where vegetarianism had yet to catch on, the phrase 'She knows her onions' was frequently bandied about in reference to me and a couple of people took to referring to me as 'Lettuce Galore, Pussy Galore's vegetarian cousin'. *The Cranks Recipe Book* was the beginning of my culinary repertoire's widening from jacket potatoes with beans and microwaved broccoli with melted cheese.

When I passed my exams at the end of the year, I began the university entrance A-Level courses and chose Art and English Literature. The latter was taught in a cramped room, mainly taken up by a long rectangular table. One of the walls was lined with bookshelves that were bursting with tatty paperback classics which we were allowed to borrow whenever we wanted to do some extra reading. With my steady routine at a school where I was content, I gradually became able once again to concentrate for long stretches, and could now read an entire book without the jiggling knee syndrome. I began by reading everything I could lay my hands on by Lawrence and Hardy, mistaken by Manda to whom I frequently mentioned them jointly, for Laurel and Hardy, whom I also revered.

Mr Watkin, my English literature teacher, had prominent wiry eyebrow tendrils that made up for the hair he'd lost on the top of his head. Like Mr Ray, he was a crucial stepping stone on the way to my becoming a functioning adolescent. I may not have been able to write a succinct essay but ideas poured out of me in class discussion, with which he tumbled along, throwing more ingredients into the mix for me to digest. Some of the others in that class had grown long in the tooth about school, for which I had no tolerance as I was just getting back into my stride with enthusiastically appreciating what I was learning. When Hope, a girl in the literature class, declared that she didn't like Emily Dickinson 'because she had a centre-parting', I countered this by giving a passionate recital of 'Hope Is The Thing With Feathers'. She tried not to snigger at my flourish on the final line, 'It asked a crumb of me!', as she saw I was deadly serious and avoided such vapid comments in future.

Mr Watkin arranged an annual coach trip to Stratford-upon-Avon for us literature students. I had only been to the theatre a couple of times in my life. When I was about six, I was taken to a pantomime of *Cinderella* featuring soap opera stars with whom my mother was familiar. A few years later, I was brought along to a production of A *Chorus Line* in Leeds, which went completely over my young head, particularly when one of the female characters sang out, 'Tits, tits, I wish I had tits', a line which mortified my mother who attempted to cover my innocent ears with her hands. In fact, this line still baffles me today knowing, as I do, the encumbrances of being well-equipped in that area. The play we saw in Stratford-upon-Avon was *Othello* and I sat in awe for the full four hours. Afterwards, I enthused about it to Jen, a girl from a cultured background, who said it was 'rubbish' and Ben Kingsley, who'd played Othello, 'was just the same in *Gandhi*'. 'What's *Gandhi*?' I asked. She did not even bother to answer and merely turned away in disdain. When I eventually did get to see *Gandhi*, however, Ben Kingsley seemed completely different from when he played Othello, at least to my uncultured eye.

Jen was more mature than the rest of us. Just before I met her, she had left home to have a go at living in a flat with her older boyfriend, which had created a bit of a buzz around Wyndham. This had not worked out so, a couple of months later, she was back home again, bouncing along as if nothing had happened. A couple of girls didn't like her for some reason I knew nothing about. Jen used to haphazardly knit her own jumpers and, on one occasion, they managed to grab a thread of a particularly unravelling one. As she went down the stairs of one of the tall school buildings, the jumper gradually disappeared until there was almost nothing left of it by the time she reached the ground floor.

Despite my lack of cultural knowledge, Jen and I became friends and I often stayed over at her house, a four-storey Georgian building that stood alone in what looked like a crater that had once been a quarry. Jen's room was at the top, directly under the inclined slate roof and was noisy in the frequent rain. I liked going there because she had a bona fide family life, which I'd lacked for some years. Jen's mother was a kindly teacher of the deaf. She had strawberry blonde hair in no particular style and, like her daughter, almost transparent blue eyes. They had a boisterous, young golden labrador, Tyke or 'Ticky', who would leap up with slobbering jaws and lick your face, as well as whipping you with his frenzied tail. Mark, Jen's younger brother was about fourteen and had a bizarrely indifferent manner. His black hair was intricately spiked and he always dressed entirely in spotless white. I used to think he looked like an Oompa-Loompa in Willy Wonka's Television Room. He would never look away from the video game he was playing, which prompted me to attempt to engage him in conversation whenever I was there.

I often accompanied Jen to her house after school and, one afternoon, we arrived in the midst of a commotion. Mark, who was always so still and silent, was having a meltdown completely out of the blue. He had barricaded himself in Jen's bedroom at the top of the house and was raving. Their mother, standing outside the room, was worried he'd throw himself out of the skylight and was pleading with him. Poor Tyke was beside himself, charging at the locked door and howling. I spoke to Mark through the door and he finally came out and walked towards me like a zombie wanting a hug. I went along with it and then he burst out with, 'You! You, fascinating spark of light!', which were the first words I'd ever heard him speak.

We took him downstairs and made a pot of tea, the British cure-all, but inexperienced as I was, I knew that it was unlikely to help with this kind of malady. He gabbled, clinging to an idea that God was going to help him. His mother nodded her head, agreeing that there were so many nice Biblical stories with noble morals, which was the most she could do as she wasn't a church-going lady. Mark insisted that I must be part of his life too because my 'intervention was also going to be invaluable' so I started visiting the house more often. He would give me parts of the Bible that he had copied out in erratic handwriting, for which I'd thank him before he would proceed to decipher the coded messages in them, discussing how they might help him. Mark had gone in one fell swoop from a sullen, robotically introverted boy to a non-stop talker with wild eyes and tangled hair. At first, it was passed off as hormonal, a backfire in the onset of puberty. But after a few years of this mania, nothing had changed and he went to live in long-term sheltered housing.

At school, Jen had her eye on Jonty, an academic star who'd been earmarked for Oxbridge and was her intellectual equal. Jonty, however, kept a safe distance from Jen who, given her recent liaison with an older man and her being attired in a fake leopard skin jacket, indicated to his inexperienced mind that she erred on the side of predatory. To her consternation, Jonty was instead displaying signs of being keen on me, looking over at me slightly longer than was usual as I babbled on in our literature class, and often spending part of the lunchbreak with me. Jen had nothing to worry about because, in my mind, Jonty and I were engaged only in research. On most days, we'd meet up, walk to the green-grocers next to the school and buy a different variety of apple. Many of the apples had names that seemed to belong to romantic heroines: Margil, D'Arcy Spice, Genet Moyle, Belle de Boskoop and, of course, the one originating from the soil beneath our feet, the Egremont Russet. We were creating a ranking of apples and would discuss, at length, the strengths and flaws of each.

Before too long, the liaison developed into some-thing beyond apples. I went with Jonty to a few of the old-fashioned barn dances that he favoured, held in village halls with fiddlers and bales of hay to sit on. It was all very Hardyesque to me, especially in so far as, like a typical Hardy heroine, I was highly resistant to romance. From time to time, I visited Jonty at his house, where he liked to show me the very deep fish pond he'd excavated in the dead centre of his lawn. We'd stare in, waiting for one of the goldfish to appear. One weekend, we went for a walk along St. Bees beach and, feeling somewhat liberated from my nineteenth century demureness through my admiration of Lawrentian female characters, I urged Jonty to take off his shoes and socks and paddle with me in the sea barefoot in a bid to make him more relaxed. It worked, but five minutes later he put his hand on my hair and I froze. He shrugged and we walked back to his house pretending it hadn't happened. I may have been preaching a spontaneous and passionate life but I still wasn't ready for it. Trying to overcome this frigidity with the bleak tryst with the short-term boyfriend on his kitchen floor had proven futile. Mixed with thoughts of Andrea, whose potential, I felt, had been rubbed out on the back seat of her boyfriend's car and, of course, my own parents' all too lengthy liaison, probably contributed to my being so guarded and never having known a flicker of an erotic feeling.

I had often preferred the company of boys and could trace this right back to my five-year-old self, with visits to the neighbouring house of a boy called Alex who had curly locks and a runny nose. His mother had abandoned the family, yet Alex was always smiling. His dad couldn't really cope with his four sons and their house was a scruffy place, the garden like a junkyard, but what a lot of fun we had, climbing into the carcasses of cars. We tried to teach his lone chicken to fly. I would climb onto the roof of his shed and Alex would stand on the ground, arms outstretched, whereupon I'd toss the submissive hen into the air. It would squawk and flutter its baked-bean coloured plumage, falling with style into Alex's arms. We would try until the poor hen would finally hide herself under one of the cars where we couldn't reach her.

I liked to stop off at Tim's house on the way home from school. He lived in a small village on the bus route between Egremont and Whitehaven in a dormer bungalow with an immaculate lawn bordered with daffodils. Unlike Jonty though, Tim found it a bit much when I rattled on about poetry, plays and novels. However, he was interested in my artistic side because, as he liked to say, a girl with flowing raven hair in possession of a large portfolio can be quite alluring. He obliged me by sitting still for hours while I drew him and we became at ease in each other's company.

Tim and I initially wafted toward each other through our love of the same music. When I wasn't drawing, we'd sing along to Smiths songs, followed occasionally by boisterous play on a strange collapsing couch in his room. We'd eat cornflakes whilst enjoying another shared interest, the films of Woody Allen or Laurel and Hardy. Tim had a little of Woody Allen's awkward hesitance in him and it was this, along with my own qualms, that stopped our friendship becoming amorous. He'd have proper girlfriends for stretches of time during which my visits to his home would be put on hold.

There came upon me at about this time an urge to abandon my denim armor and to start wearing vividly coloured, loose and flowing clothes, influenced perhaps by my fondness for paintings by the likes of newly discovered artists such as Klimt and Chagall. I could probably have benefitted from some guidance in this as I only seemed to choose colours that clashed. Whether this was a concrete expression of lingering psychological instability, or arose from a sudden strong desire to be noticed, after striving for so long not to be, or a bit of both, I remain unsure to this day. One of my typical outfits was emerald green leggings, paired with a pink cable knit jumper, or maybe a bright yellow zip-up top.

Curiously, concurrent with this, my art changed direction. All I'd done previously were incredibly accurate, highly intricate pencil drawings of house-plants or mechanisms in household appliances. Now I took to working on a much bigger scale and my favourite subject matter was feet. Not just ordinary feet but feet the size of boulders painted in clashing bright hues like the colour palette of my new clothes. I developed such a great appreciation of feet that I was even toying with the idea of becoming a chiropodist. I imagined having my artwork on the walls all around my chiropodist's surgery, distracting my patients as I excavated their verrucas.

I looked up the grade requirements at university for such a course and they were very low, which was handy as I didn't do so well in exams because I couldn't think in an organised way under pressure. The school careers advisor, Tim's father as it happened, like the Head of Sixth Form, could never understand how I had no plan at all as to what I would do, or where I would go after school. He looked puzzled when I told him I'd decided on a career in chiropody but duly handed me the relevant prospectus to take away and read.

Meanwhile, the miraculous dancing Ferg had finished his exams, chopped off his trademark hair and taken to wearing dull ironed clothes as he had been given a job doing admin work at the school, whilst saving up for a big trip to India before going to university. I was feeling bold one day, whether it was because he no longer had his mane, or that I was in a dayglow harlequin suit, I still don't know, but we got chatting. This soon led to lunchtime sandwiches at his house, which was good as I often ran out of money. I was taken aback by the normality from which the singular Ferg had sprung. Like my childhood friend Alex, he was the youngest of three brothers and his elderly parents were typical small town Cumbrians. His dad was the archetypal flat capper, while his mum was an old lady in an apron with a grey perm who might've been one of Manda's friends. This reminded me about how differently so many people turn out from their parents.

Since his 'Let's Evolve!' days, Ferg had become more subdued, more serious, with me mainly being the joker when we were together, which was fitting as I was dressed like Harlequina. Ferg turned out to be vegetarian too. He made a top cheese and salad sandwich and was among the kindest and most generous hosts a scatty seventeen-year-old in mismatched clothes could ever hope for. I repeatedly promised him I would take him out to dinner one day to thank him for all his sandwiches when I could save up enough money.

My father had been commanded by the family court to send me fifteen pounds per week pocket money, which my mother wanted me to use for clothes, toiletries and vegetarian novelties outside the house. It was a challenge, even in the distant 1980s, to make this amount last the week so I decided to try once again to get a job. My first experience at Benny's wasn't one I wished to repeat so I applied for a Saturday 'counter job' advertised in the window of the supermarket near my house and was asked to come in for a trial. Convinced I would be assigned to the warm and sweet-smelling bakery section, where I'd hand warm loaves to smiling customers and fill little cardboard boxes with dainty cakes tied up with ribbon, I was quite excited. Alas, the manager showed me to the deli counter where he proceeded to teach me how to use a large, frightening, stainless steel meat slicer. I wanted the extra money though, so I accepted the work, horrified at what I was doing by the animal rights leaflets I regularly picked up in the library about cruelty in the meat industry.

Eight Saturdays later, I could do it no more. The first thing that had really shaken me was tongue. I'd been given tongue in sandwiches when I'd visited May's as a child but somehow it had never occured to me that tongue was from an actual tongue. I think I'd always thought that it was called that as it was something you put on your own tongue. Opening a gigantic tin of tongue and shaking out the slippery cylinder, I was aghast to see four or five giant cow tongues suspended in jelly, which magnified their texture with graphic detail. I then had to negotiate this slippery block onto the slicing machine and cut it into wafer-thin slices, which gave me the shivers while I pressed my own tongue firmly to the roof of my mouth, as if it might shoot out at any moment and be sliced off by the machine.

Something else that disgusted me was how bad I smelled after a day's work; it was a combination of blood, smoked meat and animal fat. When I got home, I'd stand in the shower until the hot water ran out, comparing myself to Lady Macbeth trying but failing to get rid of the spots of blood on her hands. Sometimes I'd speak a few of her lines, 'Here's the smell of blood still!', whilst referring to my bargain shower gel as 'the perfumes of Arabia'.

Having finally saved some money, I was at last in a position to offer Ferg a thank you for all the eating I'd done at his house, as well as his having bought me many a bar of chocolate. We met in a little Italian bistro in Whitehaven. The waiter came over and lit the candle on the table for two and popped a red rose into the vase. Inwardly, I panicked, wondering if this could be misconstrued as a date. Halfway through the meal, two boys from Wyndham walked by. I waved them over and offered them some garlic bread. Ferg rolled his eyes; he'd obviously thought it was a date. After the meal, I invited everyone up to my place to watch a video but Ferg politely declined my invitation and said something about hoping I'd have given him at least one hug tonight before he jogged away. As I watched him go, I had mixed feelings. On the one hand, I felt like I'd escaped from a bona fide date while on the other, I felt monstrously callous. How could I have done this, not only to Jonty, but now also to the Ferg, who'd evolved into this complex being whom I had just repelled? It occurred to me only then that I'd been happy to soak up admiration from boys, but I hadn't ever considered how they'd feel when I turned them down.

The next time I saw Ferg was some months later upon his return from India. Generous and kind as ever, he brought me a pink Indian suit with an embroidered neckline which I kept for years until I wore it out.

8

Lord Byron's Illegitimate Descendent, an Instructive Tale

Jen had got herself a new boyfriend and she told me he looked like Jeremy Irons. We'd seen Mr. Irons in *Richard II* at Stratford that year and, being on the front row of the stalls, some droplets of his spittle had rained down upon us during one of his emotional speeches, which we didn't mind in the slightest because we were besotted with him.

I met Hugh, Jen's new boyfriend, in The Puncheon Inn, which was down a back alley in Whitehaven. He had long straggly chestnut-brown hair, dark deep-set eyes and chiselled cheekbones...all in all, a passing semblance to our favourite thespian mixed with a smidgen of Plains American Indian. She sat wrapped around him in her trade-mark fake leopard fur coat and he referred to her as 'my big pussy cat'. He was stylishly dressed in a flowing, dark wool coat, cashmere scarf and leather boots. He looked every inch how I expected an actor to look and I suddenly felt a bit silly in my clown-bright colours.

I recall little of what was said other than him talking a very great deal about himself, how he could wear anything and still look fashionable, such as my whimsical attire, or even a bin liner. His vanity led me not to take much of a shine to his character but I found him agreeable enough to look at. A week after this meeting, Jen had resolved not to see him again. She told me that she had decided he had never actually been her type. In fact, she said, he had told her that I was more his type, and had asked her to give him my number. This struck me as peculiar but she didn't seem bothered. Hugh rang me a few days later and I thought I'd give 'a date' with him a go.

We met at the entrance of Castle Park in the centre of Whitehaven and ambled over to his house. There were some feeble attempts at conversation: he was scientifically minded and off to do a physics degree that year. When I tried my usual talk about Shakespeare, in spite of his actorish good looks, he had stifled a yawn. Eventually, we came to a mansion with monumental stone columns and wrought iron gates which he began walking towards.

'Is this really your house?' I asked, hanging back.

He laughed, 'No, just kidding.'

We walked on for a while but then he grabbed my hand and took me back through the gates with him. 'I actually do live here. No one ever believes me at first.'

For a few minutes, I thought I might be in the company of an aristocrat from whose generous hands great largesse might fall upon me but, alas, this mansion was now the offices of the water board and Hugh's father was the live-in caretaker.

Their residence was a little flat in the attic with pitched ceilings. Hugh made me some tea in the compact kitchen. When his friendly father came in, Hugh rolled his eyes, which his dad saw but he kept

115

on smiling. His dad was smaller than him and with a very different manner, obligingly answering all my questions about how old the house was and what its history had been. I was amazed to hear that it was Hollins Mansion, the very place where Manda had been sent to work as a maid at the age of fourteen. The same building was later used for long-stay convalescence. In fact, my father had stayed there when he fractured his skull after going over the handlebars of his bicycle at the age of nineteen. My mother had often said that it had been this accident that had changed his brain and made him into a far worse person, even though it was probably that he was simply a narcissist who was charming to people at first, but took them for granted once he felt he had firmly secured their affections.

The sloping ceiling in Hugh's room was so low that he could only have a mattress on the floor. There was a rosy shade on the table lamp and he put on some subtle pulsating music but, try as he might, it was no use, I felt not a jot of desire for him and no clothes were removed in the attempt. During all this, I remembered Manda telling me that the servants' quarters had been in the attic of Hollins and I wondered whether this had been her very room. I imagined, sometimes aloud, even though Hugh was uninterested, how she got up with the crowing of the cock to go downstairs and sweep the grates and light the fires. An hour later, I was trotting over to Hensingham with only one thought in my mind, 'I can't wait to tell Manda that I was in Hollins Mansion!'

For some reason, Hugh had been referring to me

around town as his new girlfriend. I hadn't seen him for a couple of weeks and we had only chatted briefly on the telephone with me giving a vague promise that I'd meet him in a pub sometime soon. I was in Whitehaven town centre on a Saturday and, as is the way with small town centres consisting of two streets of shops, you bump into everyone you know. Hugh suddenly popped up and put his arms around me in a stiff embrace. Next to him, however, stood Percy Bysshe Shelley, or someone quite similar anyway, in a yellow paisley waistcoat, a Tootal cravat and oxblood brogues. His hair was a sort of pale apricot and his eyes, copper brown. He was introduced as Marcus and when he smiled, he revealed fang-like canines. For someone transfixed by the literature of the Romantic Period, this was an intriguing moment. I even fancied that I looked similar to Byron and occasionally told people that I was probably descended from an illicit affair he'd had with a Cumbrian dairy maid making me, in all likelihood, his many times great grand-daughter.

I spent the rest of the afternoon mainly talking with Marcus as the three of us wandered about the blustery harbour. We sat on one of the sea-eroded sandstone walls and eavesdropped on a conversation between two of the native trenchcoat men which ran thus: 'Ave you got a new dog, marra? She's a beaut, is'n she? What's 'er name?' To which the other fellow replied, rather uncomfortably, 'Beaut'. Marcus and I found this a hoot but Hugh was too aloof to giggle along with us, sneering and referring to them as 'Dumbrians' and looking forward to the day he left the 'Godforsaken place' for university.

Marcus poked fun, in a friendly way, at the oranges and lemons colour scheme I was wearing. It may have been light-hearted but it must have touched a nerve because the following week, in a bid to update my look in line with his, I caught the train to Carlisle and visited the shop he had told me about, Daisy's Antiques, along with the local charity shops, many of which had cheap antique clothing.

The next time Marcus saw me, I had transformed into Jane Burden, wife of William Morris and mistress of Dante Gabriel Rossetti, in a long grey dress with a black shawl, brown lace-up boots and a little black velvet tam o'shanter with a silky tassel. Enchanted, he began meeting me in old-fashioned cafes for Lapsang Souchong from china teacups and thus our faux antique courtship began.

He was a monologue man and his outlook was not one I was familiar with: highly articulate, filled with existential despair but embellished with humour, albeit dark. He knew more than I did, and even more than the daunting Jen, about literature and art. We'd go to the library and browse through books together, as if we were taking a break from shooting a period drama of a late Hardy novel. He loved the Pre-Raphaelite paintings and showed me which models reminded him of me, including one of the tempt-resses in *Hylas and the Nymphs* luring the unfortunate fellow to his death in the water. I visited him at home a few times at his grandparents' tall terraced house in the town centre. His room was on the top floor and lined with bookshelves. He had gone to live there a few years previously because he wasn't able to get along with his down-to-earth

Cumbrian parents, whereas his grandparents put up with what any sensible girl might have realised were his pretentious idiosyncrasies.

When I'd known him for a month, he slipped into the conversation the shocking revelation that he'd had to leave his school after he'd struck another student over the head with a hammer. It had not been an accident and the whack had knocked the boy unconscious. After this, he'd been sent to counselling for his mental health and had been diagnosed as psychotic, which was why he was doing his schooling by correspondence. He was also, he casually mentioned, engaged. She was a naive girl from his old school who'd recently applied to do a primary school teaching qualification.

It struck me, at that point, that there might be a reason he'd got together with someone who liked looking after small children but I foolishly dismissed the intuition. He told me that I was his heart's desire but that I wasn't good for him in the way that his fiancée was. She enabled him to function, he said. He was now going to stop seeing me because she had found out about all the time we were spending together and was hurt by it even though we'd not been at all passionate. She had agreed with him that a 'femme fatale' such as myself was no good for him. I liked the old films noir and was taken aback by the blatantly ludicrous comparison of my guileless self to a femme fatale but, at the same time, I felt complimented and thought of adding a characteristic black veil to a 1920s cloche hat I had lately bought at Oxfam. I was the one who had been tempted by him, and had childishly changed my image to seek his approval, though I had to say, I preferred my new muted tones and natural fabrics to the dayglow synthetics I had sported hitherto. So, we broke it off, whatever 'it' had been.

A few weeks after that, there was a sixth form Christmas costume party held in a beautiful old country house called Lynthwaite Hall that had statues of the muses outside. I put together a few things I found in the charity shops and, snipping and stitching here and there, created a passable Alice in Wonderland dress. There was a lot of drinking, loud music, the odd flash of nudity, then Tim dressed as a cowboy rushing over to me and telling me he needed to speak to me outside. I duly followed him to the car park wondering what on earth was the matter.

'I just want to say,' he said, swaying, 'I just want to say, I really, really, really like you,' and then, turning greyish, he bent over and discharged the largest amount of vomit I'd ever seen.

I thanked him and turned sharply to remove myself inside.

'I feel like more than a friend with you,' he called after me, 'Isn't it the same for you?'

Confused and thinking I may not have conducted myself properly with him on his collapsible couch, I continued walking. Once inside, I damped down this guilt by going directly to the bar, buying a pint of lager and having a few gulps as soon as it was set before me. Lager in hand, I turned to see Marcus entering the room dressed as a sinister clergyman cast as a villain in a melodrama. He wore a wide-brimmed black hat and, under a three-quarter length jacket, his shirt was on backwards to imitate a clerical collar. Walking over to me, laughing, he said I looked 'Ravishing, absolutely ravishing, Alice Liddell with a pint!'

'And does your fiancée know you've come here seeking diversion?' I asked him.

'Of course not!' he chortled, 'I sneaked out.'

'Crikey, it's like you're in an asylum and she's your mental health nurse.'

'Yes, it is and that's just what I need! Women like you are bad for me!'

'So why the hell did you come to this party dressed up like a wicked vicar?'

'Don't you see, you lured me here!'

'No I did not!'

I was unsure if it was because I was tipsy or because he was in villain's attire, but there was an odd little feeling stirring in my loins which I thought could possibly be passion. Soon after this, we had a bit of a cavort on the dance floor to Doctor and the Medics' cover of 'The Spirit in the Sky', followed by fervent osculation in a dark corner, but his canines were a little on the sharp side. Perhaps he was a reincarnation of those pompous men of the cloth who had written the admonitory chapters in *A Young Lady's Miscellany* rolled into one of the cads they were warning girls like me about.

An hour later, walking entwined across the car park to catch the last bus back into Whitehaven, I wondered what on earth I was letting myself in for with this unhinged, bogus man of God.

A group of boys drove past us in a Mini, one of them shouting out of the window, 'Give her one for Christmas'. I heard Tim laughing in the back.

Perhaps his despair had turned to resentment on emerging from deep to shallow drunkenness. The Mini then turned back and drove in a circle around us, this time with someone shouting 'Give her two for Christmas'. They kept on driving around and around us until they got to eight and sped off.

Following his forbidden outing, I received a book through my letterbox wrapped in Christmas paper, an anthology of dreams with an inscription in the front, *All my love, Marcus xxx*. All his love, I mused, none left for the naive fiancée? And three kisses?

There was to be a school production of *Hamlet*, which we were studying for our final exams. I offered to make the poster. Again, the metamorphosis of my exterior had mysteriously redirected my art: I was now foregoing bright colours in favour of charcoals and inks. I found a dead jackdaw and brought it back to my mother's flat, placing it on a sheet of newspaper upon the kitchen table. Without pondering for a moment the hygenic consequences of such an action, I set to drawing it in a grey ink wash, thinking that was the perfect illustration for a production of Hamlet inspired by the line, 'Come, the croaking raven doth bellow for revenge', with the late jackdaw standing in as a lesser raven. An hour or so later, an accomplished drawing was emerging when Marcus rang the doorbell. I hadn't seen him since the Lynthwaite Christmas do.

'Look, I really shouldn't be here,' he explained as he followed me into the kitchen, 'You know, you're bad news, bad news for me but I was just passing and I couldn't stop mysel— Why the hell have you got a dead crow in your kitchen?!'

I told him it wasn't a crow, it was a jackdaw and he soon calmed down. He then sat watching me draw, all the while chattering on about his dilemma of being engaged to a sensible person but, at the same time, being smitten with me, whom he referred to as his 'temptress', which I thought was stretching it. Was he making up a story for himself, I wondered, to make his dull life more exciting? Suddenly, a wriggly little grey thing burst out of the jackdaw carcass and shot off the table. With an animation I'd never seen in him before, Marcus leapt up and stamped and stamped on it until it was more than dead. Remembering his psychotic diagnosis and the boy he hit with the hammer, I was relieved when he had to dash off to meet his fiancée for afternoon tea.

I decided to audition for *Hamlet* but I had never been in a play, and had barely set foot in front of an audience. The prospect daunted me but I was ready to have a try. A disastrous public appearance had occurred in primary school when I was aged about seven. I hadn't memorised 'The Holly and the Ivy' on my recorder for a performance at the Christmas show where I was to perform with two other little girls. I had the idea that if I just moved my fingers about, no one would notice. The only problem was, I blew into the instrument at the same time and made the noise of a snake charmer which, unfortunately, everyone noticed apart from me. So, it came as a surprise, in the wake of this impressive debut performance, to be given the part of the tragic waif, Ophelia, with whom I identified to some extent. Her line 'Woe is me!' just prior to her descent into madness, was a reminder that I should never slip into feeling too sorry for myself lest the same happen to me. I went to the library to look up artists' impressions of Ophelia to get costume ideas. Lizzie Siddall in the river, waiting to be drowned by her waterlogged, yet exquisite garments in the Millais painting was lovely but too ambitious for my mother at her sewing machine.

Jonty had been given the part of Claudius, uncle and stepfather to Hamlet, but felt miffed because he'd wanted the leading role. We had all thought he would get it but Mr Watkin had picked a string bean of a boy who'd never done any acting before. Of course, Gertrude's line 'He's fat and scant of breath' is a clue to Hamlet's physique, which didn't fit with Mr Watkin's choice of actor at all, whereas the more rounded Jonty would have been perfect. Furthermore, Hamlet is supposed to be about thirty which was another point in Jonty's favour as he was occasionally mistaken for a teacher when we were out together sourcing apples, whereas the lad picked to play Hamlet barely looked fifteen. Jonty had hoped that 'playing The Dane' would be the grand finale to his school days and was always a little jaded in rehearsals.

To develop our acting skills, Mr Watkin would often show us an extract from an excellent series, *Playing Shakespeare*, with its opening credits of a revolving Bard-bust accompanied by enthusiastic Elizabethan fifes. It was presented by John Barton, a Royal Shakespeare Company director, bearded and attired in a cardigan and knitted tie, at which Jonty and I always sniggered. The series was filmed in a casual workshop setting with actors lounging around, drinking tea and smoking, making me think, *hi-diddle-dee-dee, an actor's life could be for me.*

Mr Watkin's wife, a supply teacher, would help us warm up for rehearsals with unusual exercises of her own devising. One of these she introduced as 'Pieces of Paper Blowing in the Wind' in which we were to follow her lead in gusting about the room. The problem was, that the sight and sound of her in her clodhopper shoes, like Frederick Ashton in his famous clog dance, didn't lend a great deal of grace to her performance as she blew about.

Mr and Mrs Watkin were a generous couple and opened up their house to a load of teenagers for a party to celebrate being mid-way through their drama production rehearsals. There was a buffet and a punch bowl. Going home from this event, I embarrassed myself by slipping down their icy steps, while the Watkins looked on with concern from their doorway. I made a hasty exit in case I teared up in front of them because the pain was excruciating. Afterwards, a bruise appeared on my left buttock which looked like a map of Africa. It was so accurate, I even showed my mother, who agreed.

We were expected to provide our own props in addition to our own costumes and I needed flowers for Ophelia's famous 'mad scene'. I didn't have the money for fresh flowers so I considered getting them from the bin in the graveyard, but had received some suspicious looks when I went to investigate. I then remembered that May could make all manner of items, probably including artificial flowers so, after school one day, I decided to walk up to Hilltop Road. I hadn't seen May for a few weeks, preferring these days to be out with friends on a Sunday, rather than participating in family get-togethers in the old parlour tradition. I knocked tentatively at her door, which was opened, to my horror, by Jim chewing upon some meaty repast. Hesitantly, I asked if I could see May.

'Come in, come in,' he beckoned, the friendliest I'd ever seen him.

May was just finishing off her meal and hastily cleared the table, pleased both to see and to help me. We sat together making flowers out of crepe paper with stems made of wire wrapped in green paper tape. Jim's friendliness had been a flash in the pan, however, as the rest of the time I was there, he stayed up in his room reading the paper where, no doubt, he muttered bitterly to himself about the state of the world.

Rehearsals for *Hamlet* continued for two months. I was so enthralled by the play that I memorised great swatches of it and was able to serve as prompter whenever anyone forgot their lines. Mr Watkin had somehow managed to procure a couple of genuine human skulls to be held aloft in the 'Alas, poor Yorick' scene. These were placed on the ground for the following scene, the funeral of Ophelia, in which a scuffle takes place between Hamlet and Laertes. Attempting to inject yet more energy into the performance on the final night, a skull was trodden on during this fight, which resulted in a bone-splintering crack. Although I was meant to be playing dead, I peeped at what had made the audience gasp, which then made them laugh. There was another faux pas when the boy playing Polonius added so much talcum powder to grey his hair, a cloud of it appeared above him whenever he walked.

Being in that school play helped me in the usual ways. I became more confident about speaking in front of an audience and I learned the basics of acting. More than that though, I achieved a degree of psychological insight and, on the last night, during 'the mad scene', I suddenly felt tears on my cheeks, which was a revelation after only ever crying alone, and very occasionally, for so many years in order to not make a spectacle of myself.

I couldn't help but see similarities between my father and Ophelia's father, the self-seeking and dismissive Polonius. If the phrase 'Get back in your box' had been rendered Shakespearean, perhaps something like, 'Return thee to thy coffer, go!' it would have been credible for Polonius to say it to his daughter. For me, Ophelia, like the characters played by Louise Brooks and Lilian Gish in silent films, was another young woman in a far worse situation than I, who served to heighten my resolve to forge on.

The following month, May had a stroke that took away her ability to speak, apart from the use of expletives, which burst out when she became frustrated. A bed was set up for her in the parlour so she wouldn't need to struggle on the stairs with the sole bathroom in her house being on the ground floor.

Jim and my mother, accompanied by their sibling, Derek, decided to get together for a discussion about 'what to do with her'. When this conference took place, May was sitting up in her bed in the parlour wearing one of her knitted bed jackets. I was next to her on a wingback armchair, while her sons and daughter had retired to the hallway and shut the door. May craned her neck to listen as their voices went from murmuring to heated. I felt awful for her being able to hear them so I asked her if I could get her anything in a vain attempt to distract her. She hushed me with her hand. It was tragic that her children were making plans on her behalf behind closed doors, while she was frantically trying to catch a word of what they were saying. This will always be one of my saddest moments, seeing an old person not having a part in deciding their future. I guessed that my mother and Derek had withdrawn like this because of the pugnacious and mercenary Jim. They were likely trying to protect May from witnessing an unpleasant scene in which they had to discuss the sale of her house to cover the extra fees at one of the nicer old people's homes; Jim, meanwhile, protesting that he wasn't ready to move out.

Until the house was sold, my mother and Derek shared the surplus cost of a better care home pleasingly decorated in an old-fashioned style with barometers, framed prints of shire horses ploughing fields and mock Tudor beams. At the age of ninety-two, it must have been nice for May to have a warm en-suite room, but I felt she was still sad to leave the house where she'd lived for over sixty years, raised four children, and where there was a connection to her husband. Still concerned about her present-ation, she wore a tailored dress every day, but had to ask my mother to pluck the grey bristles from her chin as she was no longer able to do this herself.

After I finished my school exams, I heard there

was a lot of work to be had at the hotels in Grange-Over-Sands, a nearby holiday hotspot favoured by the over-seventies. Concerned about how to save some money during the two month stretch before I left for college, I wrote to a few of these hotels and got an answer back from one to come over and start immediately. So, I took the scenic train ride down the Cumbrian coast to Grange-Over-Sands and walked up the hill to The Grand, which was indeed, or rather once had been, grand. It was an enormous nineteenth century stone building with around fifty bedrooms, all of which were in need of an update. I was to be a maid of all work in the tradition of Manda: waitress, chambermaid, dish-washer and laundress. I could tell immediately that I was going to be given quite a run for my meagre money.

The manager was a cheerful lady in her thirties, with a mask of make-up and a lumbering walk which I was soon to learn was due to her not moving very often from her office chair. She took me down a staircase that led deep into the bowels of the old building where, appropriately, there was a smell of drains. Here the servants resided, sharing two bathrooms. We walked along a dismal corridor with a stained carpet and she found me a vacant cell with a steel-framed bed. There was no window, just a bare lightbulb hanging from a dusty wire. I resolved, at that moment, to try and leave as soon as possible. I would stay one month, which would earn me enough to get through the rest of the summer holidays with a bit to spare when I started college.

In the mornings, I was one of a handful of girls bringing breakfasts to the hundred or so pensioners seated in the large dining room, prior to their mid-morning strolls along the windswept northern English seafront. After this, the cooks and waiting staff would all sit around a large table together and eat the leftover breakfast fare. They were a sorry crew and all lived in the dismal rooms below. The restaurant manager, a conceited middle-aged man with a blonde perm, insisted on playing an awful tape of 1970s disco covers over the loudspeakers. The old folk complained about it because it wasn't their generation's music but he'd have none of it, saying it encouraged them to eat up their breakfasts quickly and get on their weary ways. The old toothless chef told me in confidence with a wink, that he had once killed a man. As he said this, I looked down, dubiously, at the joint he was carving. Finally, there were half a dozen younger ones, skivvies like me, all in their late teens, but with no qualifications and no prospects, as had been the case with me only three years earlier.

Something that made we wince was that these younger ones were all shagging each other in those nasty little rooms in their free time. One of the girls had laughed about her sexual partner flexing his minuscule muscles in the mirror before he got down to it with her. I found this sad, rather than funny, and cringed.

During one of our communal staff breakfasts, I reached for my second piece of toast and one of the young men laid his hand upon mine and told me not to have more as I might 'spoil that gorgeous figure'. I took it anyway and ate it with extra butter. After a week of being there and still happily unshagged, the blonde perm restaurant manager asked me in front of everyone if I was a virgin. 'No,' I replied, 'I'm a Leo.'

After breakfast, I had to go upstairs to clean a dozen or so rooms in a short space of time as there were always outgoing and incoming coach loads of pensioners. The turnover rate was so rapid because Grange-Over-Sands was regarded as a cheap two day stopover on tours around the Lake District. I found changing bed linen exhausting and occasionally had a quick lie down on one of the beds when it was just me working on a corridor.

My couple of hours of daily free time were taken up with milling about on the promenade which was, by that time, teeming with pensioners. I felt desperately lonely in that miserable place, but would watch the many species of wading birds doing their funny walks over the mud flats, which lifted my spirits. In the evening, I'd be back in the dining room serving three course dinners to the pensioners at the tables with the same terrible disco music dribbling from the loud speakers...'Ah, ha, ha, ha, stayin' alive, stayin' alive' a Bee Gees impersonator belted out as elderly gentlemen requested extra cream on their crumbles. Afterwards, I'd make my way back to my dismal room, lock the door, put the chair in front of it for good measure and try to go to sleep between the threadbare sheets that were sent down to the basement after having been worn out by the pensioners in the hotel rooms above.

It was a relief to get back onto the scenic train after a month with my small wage in my pocket. As it trundled back up the coast, I looked out of the window at the pecking shore birds whose names I had now learned: the oystercatcher, the curlew, the sandpiper, the dunlin and the lapwing, also known as the pea-wit.

A week before I left for college, I visited May, hoping it wouldn't be the last time I ever saw her. I tried to dress up for her, wearing a blue old-fashioned blouse I'd bought that had slightly puffy sleeves, buttons at the back and an embroidered front, similar to the fashions of her own teenage days in the nineteen-teens. She was most pleased with it, feeling the fabric and examining the buttons, which seemed to be in lieu of more modern demonstrations of affection such as a hug or holding hands. She still couldn't speak but smiled as she listened to me talking about the course I'd settled on, English literature, and not chiropody. When I left, I did a rare thing which I'd never done before with her. I bent down and kissed her on the cheek and she gave me a lovely smile. It struck me now how small her pale head was, how wizened her frail frame, and what a shame it was that I'd been so nervous of her growing up.

9

The Mollycoddle Institute for Immature Females

Just before I went to college, my mother rehomed my dog. It was the logical thing to do because she worked full time, while I would be moving hundreds of miles away to live in halls of residence. I felt like I'd let Jess down. She could always sense my sorrows and just having her next to me made me feel better. Now she was being thrown over so I could get on with my life. Still, it was better than being told she'd 'gone to live on a farm in the country', always a euphemism for heaven. I was assured she was going to the house of my mother's friend in nearby Workington where her husband was home all day which would be company for Jess.

Still feeling bereft, I was driven with all my worldly goods on to the next stage, not knowing whether this was the right thing to do, but going along with it as I had no better alternative. On arrival, I was shown to a miserable little room at the end of a long, windowless corridor of about twenty similar miserable little rooms. The shared toilet and shower cubicles were all the way down at the other end of the corridor. My mother, sensing my disappointment, was quick to take her leave. Perhaps she thought I might change my mind and ask to be driven back.

Other young women, if they could be so called, were being dropped off by their parents, or entire families. Some of the members of these farewell parties were weeping as if their young children were being put on the train during the great evacuation of London during World War II. I immediately felt as if I had been dropped off at a boarding school where I wasn't going to progress towards becoming an adult at all, but would instead be going backwards into a cosseted environment rife with coddled peers. This sense of coddling intensified when I gradually realised that the college I'd chosen was mainly populated by girls, due to the main courses offered being teaching, arts and humanities. Given the gender of those who generally opted for such subjects, boys were few and far between and the ratio was strongly in their favour.

Soon after arriving, a small lad with a squint got himself a glorious looking girlfriend who referred to him as 'Hot Tap' which was, I was told, a reference to their shared bathing sessions. Another boy whom I chatt-ed with occasionally in the lunch queue, abruptly told me one day that he was 'spoken for', despite my not having any inclinations in that direction. Such a phrase might have appeared in A Young Lady's Miscellany, probably with the advice that 'Young men who are in possession of a prior claim, should not be bantered with in refractories.'

I sent a letter to Jonty, expressing my dis-appointment and imagining that his rooms at Cambridge must have balconies with French windows, old oak furnishings and glorious views of Medieval architecture to which he replied, *What can I say? I am writing this letter on a mock teak and formica table, circa 1970, in a room where a cat would sustain severe head injuries, if swung. As for the 'glorious view', my room has a truly magnificent prospect overlooking the characterless college bar. Herds of drunken rugby players sweep across the plain at 3 am, a sight surely equal to any seen in the game parks of southern Africa.* Jen, on the other hand, had gone to art school in Carlisle and reported that she had made a giant red fabric cocoon within which she had lain for hours so she seemed to be in a good place. Tim had stayed on at school to do resits and felt lonely, already looking forward to when we'd be back for the holidays. In these first months of separation, we all wrote to each other regularly, having realised how fond we were of each other.

My first class was a disappointment. I'd picked a dramatic literature course entitled Drama from Ibsen to Chekhov and, as drama was now one of my favourite things, I had the idea we'd be up on our feet and acting out scenes from the canon of the emergent modern theatre. How disappointed I was to find that this was far from the case. When I asked the lecturer, an older Scottish lady, who was a dead ringer for Barbara Bush, then Vice-Presidential 'Second Lady' of the United States, she said she simply couldn't allow us to leave our seats or we'd 'Niver git threw the miterial'.

On my girls' boarding school wing, for that was basically what it was, I had made the acquaintance of those girls with adjacent rooms. Over lunch, my lackadaisical neighbour Claire, told me she found chewing 'such a chore' when I asked her why she only ever ate soup and bread. Soon after this, she broke a tooth on something hard in a granary roll, which only intensified her aversion to foods that required chewing. When Claire realised there was a severe dearth of boys, she had made up with her old boyfriend from her hometown and spent every weekend whisked away by him in his Ford Escort. Elspeth, a Northumbrian, was happiest in her pyjamas, in which she was usually attired when on the wing. At the first hint of dusk, she could be heard calling out 'Ooh, I love getting into my bed!' as she made her way down the corridor to her room. Elspeth was terribly homesick and scampered off to her family farm as often as possible. Another girl, Suzanne, who might as well have been called Laura Ashley as she would only wear clothes with that name in the label, hated the girls' school vibe so much that she applied for another university and was gone by Christmas.

Probably the most eccentric was Becky, who wore stiff triangular skirts, made for her by her mother, usually in a pillarbox red felt-like material. She was never seen without a prominent plastic hair clip which we referred to as her aeriel, due to its wearer being on the remote-controlled robotic doll side.

'Hi, I'm Becky,' she chirped when I first met her, 'My parents call me Becky Bonks!'

'I bet you don't,' I said to myself, 'And probably never will.'

Often the grating sounds of Becky's cello practice filled the corridor as she sawed upon the hollow

instrument between her legs. Her room had a mini-
kettle and was always enveloped in the heady scent
of artificially sweetened hot chocolate powder,
sometimes with accents of orange or mint. Concerned about her managing away from home, her over-
protective parents, who lived nearby, regularly
popped over with meals in sachets that she would
reanimate with boiled water.

Due to there being a general lack of vibrancy in
both the college and the town where it was situated,
the halls emptied out each week by Friday afternoon. On one occasion, I happily accepted an invitation to accompany Becky Bonks to her home for the
weekend. She lived in a palatial house decorated
with numerous pieces of framed photographic
evidence of her accomplishments: atop a pony in
jodhpurs, performing a deep curtsey in ballet togs,
decked out in a ski suit in St Moritz. We hadn't had
any framed photographs about the houses I'd grown
up in. Occasionally, a school photo in a cardboard
frame was propped up on top of the bureau until it
eventually slithered down the back and wasn't seen
again for a few years. Becky's family home backed
onto woodland and she had told me about the
squirrels, which were so tame that they would come
in through the kitchen window, sit on your shoulder
and take food from your hand. I certainly didn't
expect to see one of these squirrels run in and make
off with a lemon from the fruit bowl but Becky
wasn't surprised in the least when I told her.

Becky was puzzlingly passive one moment and
madly giddy the next, insanely giggly and highly-
strung, then completely unable to get out of bed in

the morning or write a sentence when an assignment was due. Perhaps it was all the chemicals in her hot chocolate powder. Somehow she got through with ingenious methods, such as the time when she hadn't read a collection of short stories and the deadline was the next day. Fortunately for her, we were often given the freedom to come up with our own essay titles so Becky, with last minute resourcefulness, decided to write about the opening sentences of each of the short stories we'd been assigned and what they lead the reader to expect, thereby cutting her required reading to about two pages. She finished the essay in a night and sailed through with a higher grade than me.

Another thing I hadn't bargained for was that the college had a popular religious studies degree so the place was crammed with fundamentalist Christians. They segregated themselves from the non-believers, walking past anyone who didn't attend the college chapel, or the services in the nearby cathedral, as if they had a bad smell, which both amused and irritated me. One such haughty Christian was Margaret, who had watery blue eyes and a helmet of black wiry hair. She used to coerce the ever-pliant Becky into attending religious gatherings. Margaret had a Christian compatriot, Deirdre, whom we privately called Dreary due to her monotone voice and etiolated aspect. I'd once made the mistake of agreeing to go for a cuppa with her in the old-fashioned tea rooms in the centre of town, where she burbled on about people in her congregation, putting me in such a stupor that it was as if the wallpaper, a tangled labyrinth of roses, were mumbling.

Dreary was another one who nudged Becky toward services so that their chaplain could boast a full house. Margaret would imbue the air with hell fire when poor Becky skipped one of the supernumerous chapel services, usually due to a late assignment, while Dreary would tut and sigh in the background, telling her there was no excuse for missing a 'Celebration of God' which, I learned from Becky, usually involved tambourines. I eventually got annoyed with Margaret and told her sternly to lay off Becky. That night, I dreamt Margaret's head was in the cupboard in my room and I was cutting slices from her cheek and eating them. A strange dream for a vegetarian and possibly one hinting at a slightly unsound mind. As it turned out, Margaret ended up having the most unsound mind of the lot of us. In her final year of college, she revealed a cancer diagnosis and the kindly college chaplain drove her to hospital every week, where he waited for her in the car park while she received chemotherapy. After a few months of this, it turned out that she didn't have cancer at all and had just been sitting in the hospital while he'd waited for her. She'd had a crush on him and wanted his attention.

Jenny, from the other end of the corridor, was a bit older and more advanced in certain respects than the rest of us. She had run away from home and joined a Christian community but, after a couple of years, had realised she no longer believed in any of it. She'd left and gone to work in the kitchens of an Outward Bound centre, where she had become an expert rock-climber. She'd also had the opportunity to enjoy the full array of muscular instructors on offer after lights out. Like me, she felt infantilised at the college, and became furious one day when Becky, on seeing a group of men in suits entering the dining room, referred to them as 'grown ups'. Jenny pined for her old active life, sexually and otherwise, as opposed to her new sedentary and celibate one, and went away with her outdoor pursuits instructor boyfriend whenever he could get time off work.

Occasionally, a male was smuggled into our cloistered corridor, which ineluctably caused a minor stir. We knew there had been a man on the wing by the tell-tale sign of a toilet seat left up, which became known as 'Codename Erect Seat'. We would speculate as to whom the phantom urinator might have been and with whom he'd spent the night. I'd never been sent to a girls' boarding school but now, here I was, experiencing all the puerile silliness of one.

Quite often, I would be the only person on the corridor for the whole weekend. I would take a walk down to the high street allowing myself a few snacks to spice up my loneliness. From time to time, I saw the ex-wife of Roger, my mother's paramour who, ironically, now lived in the same town as me with her son and his family. Whenever this happened, I'd duck my head down and, fortunately, she never recognised me. It was strange that the two females who had been a burden on my mother and Roger's relationship had both been driven off to the same distant town.

Crushingly bored, I would spend hours in the library, often sitting in one of the video booths, wearing massive padded vinyl headphones, watching old movies. I was still a fan of D.H. Lawrence, and wore out a video of Ken Russell's *Women in Love*. In hindsight, I understand that I was probably trying to fathom the nature of desire, something that was then still a mystery to me. Having been raised by parents who didn't talk about that sort of thing, and having had considerably older sisters who'd flown the nest before I reached puberty, and being too reserved to discuss the subject with more knowledgable friends like Andrea in Wales, or Jen from Wyndham, or Jenny at college, I remained almost as ignorant of these matters as the antique readers of *A Young Lady's Miscellany*. In spite of this perplexity, I was nevertheless drawn to Alan Bates as Rupert Birkin, particularly in the somewhat suggestive fig-eating scene.

It was a wonder to me, therefore, when I passed someone on the stairs on the way to a lecture who was the image of Mr Birkin, as played by Mr Bates. When I saw him a second time, I watched to see where he was going. He disappeared through a small arched door at the very top of the building, which led to the eaves where a film archive was situated. A project employing a handful of people was taking place there, in which they were copying and preserving thousands of old amateur film reels from around the county. Reality and Lawrentian fantasy became mixed up in my befuddled little mind and I boldly decided to ask Rupert Birkin to meet me. I didn't know his real name so I scribbled a little sketch of him, writing underneath To the Film Archive Man and pinned it to the door he always went though, giving him a time and a place to meet.

It was quite a wheeze for the other girls on the wing when they looked down from their rooms and saw him waiting there at the allotted time and place, 6 pm on the stone steps that led into one of the gardens below. With my heart pounding, I went downstairs and there he was, Alan Bates holding a bottle of red wine and two glasses.

'I was hoping it'd been you who'd left the note,' he said in a shockingly reedy little voice, that sounded nothing like Alan Bates. 'We've passed each other a few times on the stairs, haven't we?'

'Erm, yes, thank you,' I acknowledged, accepting a glass of wine and glancing up at the row of heads watching us from above.

'It seems we've got an audience,' he chortled, 'Would you like to go out of sight? I have my car just over there.'

I followed him hesitantly, feeling like a lamb to the slaughter. Was I really about to get into the car of a stranger? What about all those government information films when I was in primary school? Fortunately, it all turned out well because Robert, not Rupert, had a couple of tickets for a cracking production of Ibsen's *A Doll's House* from 'a theatre friend' of his. I liked the idea of hob-nobbing with these 'theatre friends'. We drove over to the play-house and, after the excellent play, had a few drinks in the theatre bar where none of the expected theatre friends materialised. He then asked if I wanted to go to his flat.

'Don't worry, your virginity will remain intact,' he promised.

My best theatrical laugh failed to mask my

surprise. How on earth did he know? Did I come across as so virginal? And what exactly did that caveat imply?

He lived in a tiny corner of a monumental stone house that had been divided into flats. When we arrived, it was absolutely freezing and ice lined the inside of the window panes. Robert turned on an antiquated electric fire that squatted in the imposing fireplace. The room was shabbily furnished and the carpets were worn thin.

Robert told me an older actor called Graham owned the flat and he rented a room from him. Graham was away playing Lear in Wales. He'd never been lucky with more lucrative television work and was slogging around regional theatres, which was hard for him now as he was over sixty. Robert told me that when Graham had been shown around the flat by an estate agent five years ago, he had felt it was familiar somehow. He later realised the house had been his imposing family home when he was a small child with affluent parents. They had sold it over fifty years ago, and it had since been carved up into flats.

Robert and I had some midnight toast and then had a go at intimacy but his heavy stubble started giving me such a rash that I suddenly understood what it must feel like to become amorous with a hedgehog. Said stubble also had toast crumbs in it and was nothing like the soft down I supposed must grace the cheek of Alan Bates. I was experiencing not a scrap of attraction for him and felt like a naive fool. I sought to bring the canoodling to a swift conclusion by asking him about the guitar hanging from the wall, which had the desired effect. He stood up and started to strum away, showing off. Twenty minutes later, he put down the guitar and suddenly knelt before me, ominously. I leaned back.

'I just have to tell you this,' he exclaimed, 'Graham is in love with me but I haven't slept with him at all, not once, I swear it!'

'Oh, no worries,' I replied, as nonchalantly as possible, realising concomitantly that I was going to be stuck there with him for the night. He'd had too much to drink and wouldn't be able to drive me back to the college. As it was now approaching 2 am, there could be no escape by public transport or otherwise. 'Do you mind if I go to sleep now, because we both need to be at college in the morning?' I asked.

Robert courteously provided me with armfuls of bedding because the electric fire had to be turned off at night as it was expensive. Before I fell asleep, I lay there reflecting on the stupidity of my childish fantasy. I would thenceforth endeavour to be more circumspect in assessing my attraction to men. On the appearance of the blankets, an aged Persian cat had sauntered in and insisted upon sleeping with me on the couch. Now and again, it woke me up by drooling over my hand, but it was nice to be with such a silken animal, instead of the scratchy Robert.

Jenny laughed the moment she saw me the next morning, 'We thought you might have been killed when you didn't come back!'

'Did you do sex?' asked Elspeth.

'Nope,' I said, scratching at what seemed to be flea bites on my arms.

'Really?' Jenny laughed again.

'Not a sausage. Literally. My hymen remains intact. He lives with another man, on whom he was probably attempting to cheat over the other side of the fence. His dalliance with me left me stone cold, like his bloody freezing flat.'

After this, I managed to avoid Robert altogether by taking an alternative flight of stairs. I only ever saw him again from a distance, much to my relief.

Meanwhile, Jenny and I had taken to talking to 'the badger', as we called him, a first year student like us, only middle-aged. At least that was what we deduced, although it was very difficult to gauge as he had a gargantuan bramble of a beard. Through jam-jar-bottom glasses, his eyes were always furtive, peering at every detail as he bounced along in thick-soled trainers. With his unusual appearance and ambience, he had been circumnavigated by the other narrow-minded students and we only ever saw him on his own, hastening to and from his classes, wherein he was training to be a primary school teacher. In the dining room, he would eat alone, closely regarding the youthful feminine masses with his magnified eyes as he chewed.

Jenny and I had the idea, born as much from curiosity as from compassion, to take our trays over to his solitary table and request to dine with him. He was surprised and flattered and immediately started chatting away to us in his strong North Yorkshire accent. He spoke a lot, as if he'd been alone and quiet for too long. It turned out that he was thirty-six, so a little younger than we estimated, but substantially older than us all the same. He had worked ever since leaving school for the council parks service in the north eastern seaside town of Scarborough, gardening in the public areas. He was married to a lady who managed a laundrette and they had two young sons. Helping them with their homework had got him interested in becoming a primary school teacher. He was spending the weekdays in the halls of residence and going home to his family at the weekend.

Jenny and I asked him about the currant slice on his tray as we hadn't seen that out amongst the dismal offerings in the dining room that evening.

'Well, it's interesting you should mention that,' he began, 'I like to sit in the peaceful churchyard in the middle of town and I've always been intrigued by a particular sarcophagus because there's a broad crack in one side of it. I've peered into it before but it's all dark, you can't see a thing. Today, of all days, I finally persuaded myself to put my hand inside.'

'And you pulled out a currant slice?' I bantered, 'Like Little Jack Horner, only with a grave instead of a Christmas pie?'

'Yes!' he exclaimed, 'And not just one but a whole tray!'

We wondered together at how this miraculous find had come about. The best theory we came up with was that someone had pinched the tray from a baker's van as it was making deliveries that morning. Feeling overly-conspicuous with a large metal tray of currant slices in their possession, the thief, or thieves, had stashed it in the sarcophagus, probably with the nefarious plan to collect the well-baked, yet ill-gotten booty, later under the cover of darkness. After dinner, the badger, or Bruce as he was actually called, invited us to his tiny room on the sole male corridor on campus, where we proceeded to enjoy some of his freshly baked tomb cake with a mug of dark Yorkshire Tea.

One day, Bruce suddenly looked less badgerly. He had shaved off his ridiculous beard and, as if it had been a sort of prickly barrier, its absence made other students begin to approach him. Thereafter, he became quite a popular figure on campus. I think it helped that he was that bit older, not quite a parental figure, more like a younger uncle, so that, in his new clean-shaven state, the students felt he made for an interesting alternative friend. He was a jolly companion until his wife left him.

While Bruce had been away at college during the week, his wife been getting to know a chap fifteen years her junior at her laundrette who'd swiftly become her boyfriend. He told us about a terrible scene that had taken place over the weekend in which his wife had got into the new boyfriend's car and Bruce had climbed onto the bonnet to prevent her from leaving. The wife had then instructed her young man to drive the car back and forth in a bid to shake him off. Bruce had returned to college on Monday and they had agreed by telephone, a few days later, to split up amicably so as not to distress their sons. As usual, she would be at home with the children during the week but would stay with the boyfriend over the weekend when Bruce came home.

I continued to have many solitary weekends at the college, with everyone on the wing disappearing by Friday evening. Whitehaven was far away and, had I gone over there for the weekend, I'd have been on the train most of the time. Besides, I couldn't have afforded the fare, despite Manda sending me a pound whenever she wrote me one of her short letters which always ended with *Miss you popping round.* Hence, when Bruce asked me if I'd like to come over for the weekend to meet his sons, I agreed immediately as I quite enjoyed the boisterous company of young children and needed a change of scene.

He lived in a colourfully decorated old terraced house about two hours away by bus. There were a lot of ethnic tapestries and rugs. He asked me to remove my shoes on entering and handed me a pair of Morocco leather slippers. They were his wife's but she, of course, was away for the weekend. Bruce made a wholesome meal using the vegetables he grew in his garden. Ever the enterprising man when it came to saving money, he used to tour skips around his hometown with a wheelbarrow at the weekend, gathering scrap wood which he sawed up to feed the pot-bellied stove in his kitchen, on which he also did some of the cooking.

I played football in the garden with the little boys and they read me their school books. When they went to bed, Bruce asked me to sit with him in his room as he was feeling a bit blue about his separation. He then began showing me his wife's clothes in her wardrobe, handling everything with care as he laid her outfits out on the bed.

'Monica is such a stylish woman, she loves wearing pink with grey; no one understands colours like she does.'

I asked him if there was any hope he could get back together with her again and he said no, none at all because she hated him now, and always left by the back door the moment he returned for the weekend. He then asked me, quite abruptly, if I would spend the night in his bed.

'What?' I sputtered, 'Is this why you asked me to come here?' He nodded, smiling, but I was irked. 'Why me? Is it because I don't have a boyfriend? Or a family to go home on the weekends? Or that I'm not a member of the fundamentalist set? Or maybe all three of the above?'

'Well, it's probably some of those, but you're also very pretty, so what do you think?'

I was somewhere between aghast and horrified at the notion of bedding the badger, to whom I didn't feel a scrap of attraction. I felt I had fallen for a dastardly plot which was probably more about retribution than affection. I told him all this as tactfully as I could manage but couldn't hide my consternation. He wasn't at all happy about my frankness and accused me of being cold hearted. I suggested we resume our friendly terms but he was morose with me so I caught the last bus back and spent the rest of the weekend in the isolated dorms. I overheard someone asking him the following week how my weekend stay at his house had gone and he'd replied grumpily, shrugging, 'Not too bad'.

The second semester began and with it the opportunity to pick new classes, which I now did by word of mouth as to the quality of the teachers, without considering whether I was interested in the subject matter.

Consequently, I picked a course taught by Paul, a lecturer who was also a poet, and returned to being enthusiastic about literature again after the Scottish Barbara Bush had smothered Chekhov's *The Seagull* in the nest. Coincidentally continuing an avian theme, in my first class with Paul, he had read aloud a famous fairy tale known in English as 'The Feather of Finist the Falcon'. The students sat mesmerized not only by his voice, intense in feeling, but also by the sinewy, tanned forearm holding the book and his unkempt mane of wavy hair. There was definitely something Lawrentian about him and he transfixed the exclusively female class. Now I was being assigned creative writing projects and we were doing bits of improvised drama, rather than being glued to our chairs, sunk in dire monotony, as in my classes during the first semester.

Paul also hosted a debate club once a fortnight at which all were welcome so, of course, I scampered along. There was always some representation from the annoying Christian faction, with whom I enjoyed locking horns. On one occasion, they sent along Dreary to debate us armed with some hastily scribbled notes from the flock to guide her. Perhaps it was because she couldn't read their handwriting, or because her pure mind was distracted by carnal thoughts, but whenever she wanted to say 'organisms'—which was often, since the topic of the debate was evolution versus creationism—the word came out instead as 'orgasms'. In the role of moderator of the debate, Paul let this go a few times, and we shared many suppressed titters until we couldn't contain ourselves any longer and exploded in loud guffaws, at which point he finally corrected her. Dreary was mortified and blamed it on being tired. Her pasty cheeks burned with the hellfire she probably feared would consume her for this revelation of her now obviously ill-suppressed lust.

10

The Virgin's Journey,
as told to a Clergyman

Another weekend was looming in which the usual mass exodus of young women who'd never really left home was taking place. In their droves they headed to the train station. I was going to be all alone in the Halls of Residence yet again. I decided, quite spontaneously, to blow a large portion of my sparse government college allowance on a train fare to Southampton at the other end of the country.

A month prior to this decision, a letter had somehow found its way into my pigeon hole with a very sketchy address on the envelope and an orotund opening that ran: *Mayhap this letter will never reach you as your college address is unbeknown to me. However if it does, hello. It is I, Marcus, writing to you, for some obscure reason.*

In a thinly veiled plea for me to become his girl-friend instead of asking me outright, he mentioned in passing that he was no longer engaged, followed by a description of what sounded to me at the time like a highly inviting room: *I am living in the former Palace of the Bishop of Southampton, a Gothic building. My room has three pointed arch windows with leaded glass panes. I also live next to a bar.*

(*A great boon!*) I responded by dashing off a short, non-committal postcard which could still be construed as representing a smidgen of interest.

This was enough, however, to put Marcus into overdrive and a long letter appeared in my pigeon hole a few days later. Again, there was a description of his room, this time in minute detail, as if he wanted me to envisage standing within it: *Your postcard now has pride of place on my bookcase, along with a Victorian picture of an angel, some lovely images of Our Lady, two postcards of ploughs, Millais's* The Death of Ophelia *and Burne-Jones's* The Mirror of Venus. *My room presently has books and papers scattered everywhere, old Spectators, Private Eyes, Telegraph supplements. On my desk, I have a large rosary, a medallion of Our Lady of Perpetual Succour, a pile of antiquarian books, a photo of a beautiful Edwardian actress in an Art Nouveau frame and an antique magnifying glass.*

He certainly knew how to read his audience because I dashed off a lengthy reply, followed soon after by a black and white photograph of myself draped gothically over an old gravestone. No message, just his name and address on the back. One of Marcus's fellow students had brought in the post at breakfast and they took to ribbing him about his eccentric girlfriend with the 'crazed handwriting'.

Thereafter, a steady stream of letters passed between us with him admonishing me for penny-pinching by using slower second class postage. Our correspondence, both vain and inane, babbled on, mainly about Victoriana such as the ghosts haunting our respective campuses and our atavistic sartorial sense, including, I see looking back at his letters, his collection of cravats...*six are paisley and one is bright yellow.*

I often included a herbal tea bag in my envelopes, proffering a salve in response to his frequent descriptions of his drinking binges, which resembled those of twits at Oxbridge in early twentieth century novels, except that the cost of Marcus's were being borne by the taxpayer, rather than his own family: *I've been outrageously drunk every night for the past two weeks due to a bout of depression,* or better still, *Last week in our local pub, which is Irish, we had a massive food fight with Ploughman's lunches* and the topper, *On Friday night we got legless yet again and someone took photos of my friend Jim and I having a wee over the bicycle sheds, but enough of these sordid details.* He was certainly having a rollicking time down there compared to me, leading the convent life at the Junior Women's Institute, North Yorks. Chapter. The tone of his letters soon intensified: *I must see you soon, otherwise I'll turn into some kind of lemon meringue* and *Send me yourself in a large parcel so I can take little nibbles out of you whenever I feel like it*, which reminded me of my curious dream featuring Margaret the Christian.

As Miss Plumpton had wisely said in my first year at Caerleon Comprehensive, we go on all kinds of journeys...journeys to get chips, journeys from one parent to the other, journeys to a grandmother who warms up our hands, but this penile pilgrimage was making me increasingly unsettled the further I chugged down the country. I soldiered on, considering it a rite of passage, a cumming of age in which I would emerge on the other side as a fully-fledged adult, a miraculous transformation. In *A Young Lady's Miscellany*, my misadventure might've been retold as 'The Credulous Virgin', narrated from the point of view of a clergyman who had heard the tale of the aforementioned virgin: 'There are an infinite number of coxcombs, who endeavour by seductive stratagems to captivate the hearts of unworldly girls'.

When I finally arrived, after many hours on the rails, it had become dark. The train had emptied out and I was the only one alighting at Southampton in a long, black wool coat, appropriately double-breasted, topped by a sage green cloche hat. With my little antique leather suitcase in hand, I must have looked like a ghost from the past. Marcus emerged from the shadows, looking as nervous as I was, though probably for different reasons. My main feeling upon seeing him was relief because, if he'd been on one of his drinking binges and had forgotten I was coming down, I definitely would not have had the money for a hotel.

When we arrived at the old Bishop's Palace, the drinking was already in full swing in the bar next door to his room. No girls were there and it was as if the twelve or so ex-public-school boys had been anticipating my arrival for the last few hours. When I appeared, a couple of them jumped up to take my hat and coat. They invited me to sit in the middle of a large leather Chesterfield and jostled each other to get places next to me. I then held them captive as I chronicled the tedium of my journey down, with the highlights of changing trains at Crewe and then again at Swindon, where I had bought a most disheartening cheese and pickle sandwich. Marcus, all the while, sat on a wooden stool to the side, regarding the scene smugly, clearly satisfied by the others' adoration of this Pre-Raphaelite model who was all his.

Being insular southerners, they wanted to hear all about Whitehaven in the uncivilized north, the old men in trenchcoats with their greyhounds, my uncle Jim bashing his engagement ring on the pavement with a hammer, the girls who brutalized me at Richmond School, including renditions of their Cumbrian accents. Under the guise of feeling sorry for me, I received drinks, kisses and hugs. One of them invited me to try his beer then made a point of drinking from exactly where my lips had been on the rim. Marcus would periodically pipe up with 'Hey, lads, lay off my girlfriend!', but he was becoming more and more slurred and didn't notice that I was getting on with one of his friends far better than the others, who'd now moved to sit next to me on the couch.

I don't know what it was about Crispin as he was dressed in a lurid Hawaiian shirt and quite ordinary looking. Maybe he gave off some alluring odour, or maybe I'd just had too much alcohol, but I was soon smitten by him. I could feel my pupils pulse into maximum dilation when I looked at him so there was no hiding my feelings. It didn't immediately occur to me that it was odd that I'd come down to see Marcus and was instead captivated by his friend.

After being their impromptu guest speaker for a couple of hours, Crispin gestured to me and I jumped up and trotted off with him. He muttered to the others something about 'showing her the Bishop's altar around the corner'. We didn't quite make it to the altar as there was a conveniently situated broom cupboard en route, which he probably knew about. This served as the setting for the best kissing I'd done up to that point, but the alcohol may have been a factor in determining this.

We returned to the bar ten minutes later, after it suddenly dawned on me in the cupboard that I was perhaps being a tad unfair to Marcus. When we returned, Marcus dived into the space next to me on the Chesterfield before Crispin and laid his claim, drunkenly slinging his arm around me. The room then started to peter out, Crispin lingering until the very end, when he realised that I was too loyal and there was no hope for him that night. Finally alone, Marcus and I ambled off to his room.

Southampton was a renowned university so, as at Oxbridge in those days, they did not believe in providing adequate heating in students' rooms. Marcus did indeed have three picturesque high Gothic windows in his room but these were not double-glazed and the only heat source came from a tiny example of one of those old, curly cast iron radiators that resemble the fossilized rib cages of lesser dinosaurs. I crouched next to this, feeling much the worse for wear after my 'drinking sesh', as he called it. Marcus, looking whey-coloured, stood swaying next to the desk, almost knocking off his pipe rack as he attempted to hold forth. Eventually, I rose and brushed my teeth, whereupon we attempted to become amorous beneath his woefully inadequate sheet and moth-eaten tartan blanket.

'How on earth can you sleep in such a freezing room?' I asked, 'Is that why you drink every evening, so that you're numbed to the cold?'

'It's you who is cold, I'm as warm as toast,' he replied petulantly.

After a time, however, my stove was somewhat primed but it didn't help that he used gratingly laddish phrases such as, 'Come on, get the wombles out then,' which surprised me as he'd previously been so erudite. Things did not go to plan, however, as he could not, for the life of him, put on the condom. The thing just kept twanging up into the air like an elastic band. I couldn't help him as I'd had no previous experience of this myself. Marcus grappled around for the instructions on the box but he'd flamboyantly tossed it away when he'd opened it and I thought I'd seen it disappear behind the wardrobe. Eventually his futile attempts became funny, for me at least and, drunkenly giving up, we went to sleep.

I awoke at dawn with a monstrous hangover and him monstrously surly. By mid-morning, I had decided he was an utter ass and that I was going to leave. He wanted to show me The Red Lion, the oldest pub in Southampton before I went for my train and, as he had no money on him, I bought us lunch.

On my return to halls on Sunday night, Elspeth asked 'Did you do the sex thing then?'

'No, I think I am cursed to die a virgin.'

'Well join the club!' she exclaimed, 'But I'm happy about it. I don't want some bloke squirming around in my bed, much less in my you know what...!'

All Elspeth wanted was to be home with her

elderly parents, sitting by the Aga in the farm kitchen with a glass of milk fresh from the teat. Perhaps I'd have wanted that too, if I'd had parents like hers...but I hadn't and, reflecting upon the self-imposed limitations of the sheltered life that awaited her, I was glad I wasn't in her shoes.

On going to the cash dispenser the next morning, the letters OD jumped out at me on the screen. I asked Jenny what that meant, offering 'Oh Dear'? as a hypothesis.

'It's figuratively an 'Oh dear', but more literally means overdrawn,' she explained, then told me to go into the bank and grovel. My senseless odyssey to the south had left me high and dry in more ways than one.

The bank manager had a sharp suit and a manicured pencil moustache. He asked me to accompany him into a tiny conference room, pulled out a packet of cigarettes and asked if I minded if he had 'one of these'. He didn't wait for an answer before lighting up. He told me I'd been a 'very, very naughty girl' and the bank would, on this occasion only, give me a loan of three hundred pounds to be paid back within the next six months or there would be consequences in the form of high interest payments. I left the little office with reddened, watery eyes. Jenny was irate as she thought he'd made me cry, but it had been nothing of the sort: it was the stinging cigarette smoke that did it.

With the end of the first year approaching, I wondered whether I could find some indulgent person who'd give someone like me a job. I'd already had three awful jobs, not one of which I could stand for more than two months. I asked myself whether it was the jobs I'd had, or if it was just me being totally unsuited to the world of work.

I leafed through a thick catalogue of student summer jobs in the library and found a charity that not only provided accommodation and food, but also gave you a small salary and even train fare to and from the place of work. I immediately sent them a nicely written letter of application, and a few days later, received in the post details of my three month placement with a middle-aged lady called Jo who had severe cerebral palsy. Jo had been fairly mobile in her youth and had done a degree in English literature, so we had a common interest. Another aspect that piqued my interest was that, because she was married to a clergyman, she lived in a vicarage. I liked the idea of living in a vicarage and envisaged a venerable country pile, where I would take scones on the lawn and help out at church fetes wearing a sensible floral print dress. Better still, the job would see me through the summer break and wipe my overdraft with a decent sum left over.

11

Self Worth through Hard Work at the Vicarage

I'd never been to Birmingham before and getting off the train at the dimly lit subterranean station was not an auspicious start to summer. On the other hand, I was met by the irrepressibly jolly Reverend Boswell who stood out in the crowd, a veritable Anglican beacon: tall, with sparkling blue eyes, in half-mast trousers and sporting huge, grey mutton chops the like of which I'd only ever seen before on paintings of nineteenth century mill owners. I was to be one of two carers for his wife, Jo, and would receive my training from the outgoing carer, Vicky. Jo had just had an operation to help her with swallowing and we'd be driving over to the hospital first, where the Reverend said I could 'get to know her a bit', while he met with the doctors.

We followed a rabbit warren of narrow corridors floored in the compressed stone tiles of the 1800s and finally came to a four-bed ward in which Jo was the sole occupant. She was propped up in bed and braced by two metal gates. She gave a big smile when she saw her husband who explained how Jo communicated: 'no' was a look to the side and 'yes' was a direct look. If Jo wanted to say something

161

else, she would look at the pencil and paper and you would go through the alphabet until she would give you the yes look on the correct letter, thus building up the sentence on the paper. Reverend Boswell then left us, saying he'd be back within an hour.

As I sat in the chair next to the bed and looked at Jo, unable to hold up her head and unable to keep her tongue in her mouth, it dawned on me that I'd committed to a huge undertaking for which I was totally unprepared and I wondered whether I was up to the task. A girl at college had cerebral palsy and was reasonably mobile with fairly clear speech but Jo was nothing like this. I babbled on about writers I liked because she'd also done a literature degree in her youth. Probably too often, I asked her if I could give her a drink. Pointedly, she suddenly looked at the pencil and paper and we went through the alphabet many times until I had transcribed the sentence, *I'm afraid I've had an accident.* I knew what she meant but didn't know what on earth I should do. After a minute of dithering, I asked her if I should press the buzzer for the nurse to which she gave the 'yes' eyes.

Two nurses in plastic aprons hauled Jo out of the bed, stripped her and hosed her down in a shower in the corner of the room. 'She stands well, doesn't she?' one said to the other as if Jo couldn't hear. In truth, Jo was wheelchair-bound and could barely stand, her knees locked in a bent position and her leg muscles wasted.

Reverend Boswell returned and, with Jo installed in her wheelchair, we drove over to the vicarage where I was going to live for the next three months. I eagerly looked out of the window, waiting for the quaint church to appear, conjuring up the scene in my head...the characterful slanted old gravestones among yew trees and the adjacent vicarage worthy of an illustration on a jigsaw puzzle. The labyrinth of red brick streets seemed endless though, and then we were parking at the end of a cul-de-sac in front of a cube-shaped modern dwelling, 'Here we are!' Reverend Boswell announced. I was crestfallen but tried not to show it. Reverend Boswell was the chaplain at the university, not a church, and this was his allotted accommodation.

For the next week, I shadowed the outgoing carer, Vicky, who familiarised me with the morning routine, which began at 8 am when Jo would be lifted from her bed and placed onto the toilet, then washed and dressed before being returned to her bed in a sitting position. Lifting properly, from the knees, back straight, was a new skill that I soon mastered and would never forget. A breakfast of porridge and warm tea was then served, but I would have to hold her spoon as she could not, despite, in her youth, having been able to turn the pages of a book. Following this, it would be *The Guardian* Quick Crossword, which wasn't quick because Jo had to spell out every answer. If I knew the answer to a clue, I wasn't to tell her, unless she had no idea, which was rare. After that, Jo would listen to a story on a tape. She usually picked the tapes, recorded by a friend of hers, of which she had plenty. These recordings were of the complete works of Dickens, and were delivered, lamentably, in the friend's soporific monotone. While the tape was on, the carer was to do some housework and make preparations for lunch. The carers lived upstairs where there were three bedrooms and a bathroom.

Vicky had itchy feet. She was ready to finish her job, return to her home village and re-establish herself in the world of courtship. I answered the phone to her father who told me he wanted to set a time when he should collect her. She asked me 'Is it a fella?', to which I ambiguously replied, 'Erm, yes'. She darted over to the phone, only to have her hopes dashed by the voice of her dad.

The other carer, Orla Killen from Enniskillen, was a lot of raucous Northern Irish fun, who once went so far as to moon out of her bedroom window at wolf-whistling builders. I'd do a three and a half day shift, then have three and a half days off and would usually spend a day every week in the city centre. I invariably visited Birmingham art gallery with its collection of Pre-Raphaelite paintings, reminding me of my misadventure with Marcus. I wished things had gone differently, but was relieved we hadn't communicated since the Southampton debacle.

Apart from free access to the rehearsals of the symphony orchestra, the rest of Birmingham city centre I found decayed and miserable. The Bull Ring, a crumbling concrete shopping centre adorned with a two metre high fibreglass bull, was where I first witnessed adolescents giving themselves brain damage sniffing glue and luminous paint. I remember the face of a boy, fifteen at the most, sitting and opening up a tin of bright green paint like a child opening a Christmas present. He inhaled deeply, getting some of it on the end of his nose.

I stopped and stared, in shock but equally astonishing to me was that everyone else just walked around this boy indifferently, as if it were normal. Someone told me to walk on or he might hurt me when the stuff took effect. Another time that unveiled more of the dark side of urban life was when I was in the rougher part of the city centre waiting for a bus and was asked by a smiling man in a flashy car if I was 'selling'. I was confused for a moment but then realised what he meant and immediately shook my head and backed away.

One day when I was doing the crossword with Jo, her husband came in with some sweet-smelling Lily of the Valley for her and placed it in a vase on the windowsill. When he left, she spelled out to me, *I am lucky to have him*. Aware of his deep fondness for her, I replied that he was also lucky to have her, at which her eyes filled with tears.

The sad time arrived for Orla to leave. Her replacement, Nicola, was a tall, robust seventeen-year-old from Plymouth with piano key teeth who'd signed on to stay with Jo for a whole year. This was a rare occurrence as most carers were either students on their summer holidays or youngsters wanting to pack a range of experiences into their gap year so the average stay was three months. Reverend Boswell was greatly pleased because it was difficult for Jo to have a constant round of new carers. Like me when I was her age, Nicola was without any qualifications, and would be going to the local college part time to get passes in English and Maths so she could eventually train to become an auxiliary nurse. The only problem was, she could hardly read. Jo was instantly charmed by Nicola and her broad Devonshire banter. Nicola would crack jokes that I didn't understand, but had Jo in stitches. For Nicola, lifting Jo was no problem but she struggled with the crossword, which began to sound cryptic when she tried to read the clues aloud.

The time approached for my departure from the vicarage and Hannah, my replacement, duly arrived for her week of working with me as her trainer. Hannah was having a gap year before taking up her place at Oxford and had signed up to do the usual three months. She was a diminutive girl and trying to teach her how to lift Jo was nerve-racking. Hannah wasn't looking forward to living with Nicola and treated her with a condescending bewilderment that, fortunately, Nicola was unable to register. When Nicola came home from college with her first set text, *The Diary of a Nobody*, Hannah cruelly remarked, 'Well, that's a good one for you, isn't it?'.

It was quite an accomplishment for me to have completed three whole months of a physically and psychologically demanding job and I felt a buzz of confidence when my train pulled out of Birmingham New Street. I had done so well that the same charity even offered me another challenging job for next summer in a women's semi-open detention centre, which I accepted immediately. I later heard that Hannah had lasted all of three weeks with Jo.

12

The Hazards of Roaming Abroad Unchaperoned

I had signed up to spend my second year of college on the European Community student exchange programme at the University of Amsterdam. It was an opportunity that was a minority interest at my de facto girls' boarding school since most of my fellow students were timid, home-orientated and/or fundamentalist Christian. The other perk was that there was a heap of extra money called The Erasmus Grant on top of the usual government allowance so I needed no persuasion.

In September of that year, I boarded the Hull to Rotterdam ferry and sat back in my allotted reclining chair looking forward to a more exciting life as we pulled away from the dismal dock. It was only the third time I had been abroad and I was thrilled.

I'd been interested in roaming since my toddler years when I would repeatedly scale a six foot high fence and dart down the road. The neighbour would call out 'She's off again!' and my mother would rush out to retrieve me. I soon had to be fitted with an identity bracelet which I still own, a tiny silver thing with my address roughly engraved on the reverse and my name on the front. The addition of the name was important since I referred to myself as 'Oil Lo', which could be misleading and, my mother said, might possibly result in my being returned to the Chinese family who owned a nearby restaurant whose surname was Lo. I soon realised that one of the main perks of growing up, possibly the only perk, was being able to roam unheeded.

The first Dutch people I ever knowingly saw were the truck drivers loping about the ferry decks. It didn't make for the most favourable first impression of their nationality as they all had 1970s mullet haircuts and were dressed mainly in brightly coloured dungarees, like children's television pre-senters of the past. Then there was the way they were speaking the Dutch language in a very loud and gutteral manner, which left me unenthusiastic about the compulsory beginners Dutch course I had to take in addition to my English literature classes.

When we sailed into Rotterdam harbour, I hadn't slept a wink on the woefully ill-designed-for-sleeping reclining chair. I was met at the dock by an Erasmus rep, a wholesome-looking, blonde Dutch girl named Saskia who resembled one of those not-to-play-with 'World Dolls' grandmothers used to display in their china cabinets, only without the white triangular hat. She drove me over to my accommodation which, unfortunately, wasn't in the quaint city centre with its canals and old gable-roofed buildings, but in a tower block on the industrial outskirts.

Saskia took me shopping, introducing me to the local specialities with which I soon developed firm friendships: *vla* (custard in a carton), *stroopwafel* (syrupy biscuits), *drop* (salty liquorice), *vlokken* (flakes of chocolate in a box, surprisingly good on buttered toast) and so many different kinds of bread.

'Here in Holland, we love bread, we even eat it stale,' she beamed through her well-leavened rosy cheeks.

Another intriguing thing Saskia showed me was the Febo: hundreds of tiny glass doors with small chrome handles lining the walls of an open-fronted space on the main street of the neighbourhood. Behind each glass door sat an illuminated sausage, or a rasher of *speck* (bacon), or some other porky titbit for efficient Dutch people dining on the hoof. They'd drop in a coin and take out their snack, after which a disembodied hand emerging from a white caterer's sleeve would mysteriously appear from behind the scenes and, hey presto, a new sausage would be put in its place. The Dutch were delighted with the Febo and I noticed that they all did the same curious thing after the first bite: they'd wave their hand beside their ear and say *'lekker'* which Saskia told me meant 'yummy'. I didn't feel I could adopt this custom. Being a vegetarian, I went for a *kaas souffle* (cheese souffle). On biting into it, it wasn't souffle-like at all, but more like perished rubber.

'Here in Holland, a *kaas souffle* is a piece of fried cheese,' Saskia grinned.

Next to the Febo was a stall that purveyed *frites met mayo* (chips with mayonaise), outside of which stood a fine example of Dutch kitsch, a fibreglass statue of De Frites Mann. His unitary head and body was a giant carton of chips, from the lower end of which emerged chunky chip legs in round, black

Mickey Mouse type shoes. At his sides, chip arms terminated in Mickey Mouse gloved hands and, between the thumb and forefinger of one, were some frites, that *De Frites Mann* was about to pop into his mouth—ergo he was eating himself.

Saskia gave me a gift of the national machine of Holland, a bicycle. It was painted entirely yellow, even the tyres, curiously. Although it was intended for someone with very short legs, I made the best of it. The next morning, I joined the throng of cyclists as I pedalled off in the direction of the university for my first class, trying to exhibit a carefree air like everyone else. Almost immediately, however, I became muddled with the route. After a while, I decided to pedal behind a group of young people with matching scarves whom I assumed must be students at some university and fortunately ended up in the right place.

This first class was with Dr. August from Chicago, the teacher of the American Literature course who had, appropriately, a look of Mark Twain about him. His substantial grey moustache merged into the plumes of cigarette smoke his room was shrouded in. I didn't mind the fumes too much because his ramblings on American literature were interesting and he welcomed our ideas. Still, I grew to prefer the approach of the Modern European Drama teacher who, after we'd studied the works of Pinter, Beckett and Ionesco for a few weeks, gave us the keys to a little theatre to put on a play ourselves and told us that we'd be graded on that, rather than yet another unoriginal essay. The theatre was in the city centre and we would also rehearse there. The third class I took was with the deluded Dr Onoozel who taught Contemporary British Fiction and lauded the transitory and mediocre works of a handful of contemporary authors, as if he truly believed they'd attain the canonical status of Dickens. The two hours per week we Erasmus students spent trying to learn Dutch were a non-starter as most of us could not get the pronunciation and grammar right, but could just about ask for directions in the street, at which point we'd invariably be answered in fluent English.

I greatly enjoyed my cycling expeditions around Amsterdam, apart from the time an old lady jumped onto the cycle path as she hailed a tram and we both ended up in a bloody tangle on the floor. From this time onward, I was particularly careful of lively pedestrians suddenly straying off the pavement.

I liked cycling to an industrial estate on the outskirts of the city that stretched on for miles: endless chain link fences, huge cranes, silhouettes of enormous factory machinery and all totally abandoned at the weekend. With Holland being so flat, I could cover vast distances within an hour without really being aware of it. I frequently cycled to the art galleries in the city centre, marvelling at Van Gogh's wonderful impasto, a revelation after previously having seen these paintings only 2D in art history books. An American friend, another Erasmus student, was so mesmerized that, without fully realising what she was doing, she reached out and touched *The Sunflowers*, which resulted in her immediately being escorted from the museum by the security guards.

Often, I would not fully know where I was going, which didn't matter because the cycling was easy enough, but once I ended up in the infamous red light district late at night. The little old houses around the canal there had been fitted with large picture windows behind which sat women in black negligees perched on cushions, offering the human equivalent to the fast foods of the Febo. In the dim crimson glow the women looked tired out and understandably mournful, barely aware of the little gaggles of tourists taking photos and sniggering about being bold enough to venture there. Most of the women looked Indonesion and even I had the sense to realise that they'd likely been trafficked there from the former Dutch colony. Again, as at the Febo, when a woman was selected, another would almost immediately take her spot in the window, placed there by a similarly anonymous pair of hands.

The wilful innocents and Christians at the college I'd left behind across the water would have found this a little too much to cope with, along with the brisk business in stealing and reselling bicycles going on in the city. These were offered on every street for a pittance usually by emaciated people with the pallor and sunken eyes of drug addiction. Frequently, strolling around the city centre, someone would mutter, 'Hashish, Hashish' as you walked past. At a student party I attended, I'd scoffed some brownies, only to be told the next day these had actually been hash brownies. With the quantity I'd consumed, it was a wonder I'd made it home on my bike because I experienced the unpleasant sensation that my head was floating, balloon-like, at the end of a string a few feet above my body, yet keeping up with me as I cycled along.

Probably the best time I had in Amsterdam was rehearsing and performing the Pinter play in the little theatre to which we'd been given the keys, and where people would come in off the street and actually pay for a ticket. We'd managed to recruit a few mature students who were better suited to some of the roles. Many of us were particularly enamoured of a tall, blonde chap called Boudewijn, whose name none of us could pronounce properly. The trouble was, he had a steady girlfriend who was an assistant editor of Dutch *Vogue* and thoroughly looked the part, leaving us sloppily dressed students no chance. Rehearsing one of my slightly intimate scenes with him, I constantly had to remind him how to say brassiere, which he always pronounced so as to rhyme with 'cashier', even in the performances before an audience.

Following the last performance of the show, all of us cycled over to the flat of a pianist and piano teacher called Jan, who was a friend of one of the mature students in the cast. Jan was tall and blonde like Bouderwijn but not quite as dashing. I was, however, immediately smitten with Jan's appealing city centre flat with French windows opening onto a shaded courtyard. His sitting room was mainly taken up by his grand piano and he tinkled the ivories as we sang along, all drinking too much. He then played Rachmaninoff's Prelude in C sharp minor, a haunting piece, which quite transported me.

I was in a semi-recumbent position over the piano in the deep meditation of profound inebriation when I noticed that everyone else had gone. I turned my attention to Jan, over six feet tall, with his head of curly hair, a substantial nose and the typically long spindly fingers of a piano player. Not particularly attractive to me but there was something appealling in his lively eye and quick smile. At the end of the piece, he invited me to sit on the couch and, as I regarded him swigging his beer straight from the bottle, I thought it none too dignified for someone who wore a tuxedo when he worked as an occasional concert pianist and regular accompanist. I removed the bottle from his hand, placed it on the table and had a try at some impromptu passion.

I woke up the next morning in Jan's bed. He was just popping out, he said, for some currant buns. I was vaguely aware how things had developed and that something had occurred on the herringbone parquet beneath the grand piano. I had the distinct impression that it had lasted no more than five minutes in total, and that I had passed that time regarding the raw wooden underside of the grand piano, something which I'd never thought to look at before and found fascinating. I recalled little of the actual act, other than a mild discomfort. There had been no fireworks, not even so much as the sorry fizzle of a damp sparkler. So, the deed was finally done and what an absolute anticlimax it had been. Had Elspeth been there, she probably would have successfully persuaded me to permanently join her celibacy club.

It transpired, once we'd had the opportunity to converse soberly that Jan had seen the play and had been keen to meet me. He had, in fact, asked his friend to bring everyone round to his flat after the closing night expressly for that purpose.

Following coffee and currant buns in the court-yard, we went for a ride to a park, with me perched side-saddle on the back of his bike in the Amsterdam style. I'd often picked up hitchhikers myself and transported them, knees raised, on the rack of my tiny yellow bike. In the park, Jan asked me if I'd like to drive to Florence with him for a few days before I returned to England to start my summer job and, never having been to Italy, as well as being without sufficient funds to go there myself, I said yes straight away. Apparently, this trip was supposed to be with his current girlfriend, with whom he'd split up from via pay phone when he'd gone out to get the currant buns, which I felt, though I kept it to myself, was more than a little premature, and hence in keeping with our inaugural sexual encounter.

With nothing else to do, I ended up hanging around for the rest of the week at Jan's. He was a fairly affectionate yet passionless chap, whose musical accomplishments I held in high esteem, creating an inauspicious foundation for a romantic relationship, much akin to that of Dorothea and Dr. Casaubon in *Middlemarch*. In another premature move, (it had become a pattern), he took me to meet his parents who lived in a far flung, sterile suburb. They were eager for grandchildren and presented me with all manner of enticing dairy products.

Jan was interested in cutting-edge, live con-temporary classical music so we went to a couple of concerts. One of these was given by a Japanese pianist who virtually crawled into her piano in the middle of her rendition of rapid and random notes. There she proceeded to pluck the strings of the piano with long, scary fingernails, whilst emitting cat-like yowls. Apparently she'd been a girlfriend of Jan's in the past and I wondered how I could possibly compete.

We went to another such concert with an unusual pairing of a harpsichord and a drum kit. We were then invited to call out 'our favourite numbers up to thirty-five', which would somehow dictate the direction of their next improvised piece. It was all pretentiously earnest and when, after ten or so numbers had been called out, I turned to Jan and whispered, perhaps a little too loudly, 'Bingo', I was stared at sternly by a few members of the audience. Later, Jan informed me that the Dutch were presently 'leading the world in innovation in classical music' and that I mustn't 'ridicule these pioneering musicians' who daringly took 'enormous aesthetic risks'.

The following week, we left for our mini-break in Florence. Jan drove his tiny car at breakneck speed, leaning forward slightly and with a look of disdain, like someone having to run with a heavy sack of potatoes. Jan didn't get a lot of piano playing work and had to supplement his earnings with teaching the instrument so we would have only three days in Florence.

When we arrived, it was unreal to see all those famous Renaissance frescoes, in the plaster, so to speak. Unfortunately, Jan insisted on going into every one of Florence's seventy-odd churches and chapels and reading aloud the provenance of every one of them to me from his guidebook. I wanted to sit in a square having a cappuccino, or sprawl on some steps and watch the world go by, but, for him, cultural tourism was a military exercise in which conquest of every artistic objective was required.

The evenings were also disappointing. We would go to one of the characterful little restaurants and I would dress up slightly but the way Jan blew his soup using his entire mouth, like a discharging vacuum cleaner, extinguished any romantic feelings I was trying to have. Following the meal, it would be back to the city campsite to sleep upon the compacted earth.

On the second day, Jan took my photo beneath the huge statue of Michaelangelo's *David* and, as I looked up at all that unabashed phallic glory, I wondered what it was I was missing. I was given a hint of it during those three days in Florence where, to my surprise, I appeared to be standing out more as a desirable being than I ever had before, with many a devilishly handsome Renaissance youth seemingly riveted by me. Jan noticed it too and it made him uneasy, as if these hot-blooded Mediterraneans might, at any moment, successfully challenge his chilly and shaky northern European hold over me. It wouldn't have been difficult because just hearing Italian on this trip made me weak at the knees, whereas the Dutch language left me cold as a carton of pasteurized milk. I was told later on by an Italian friend that it was likely my English rose complexion and green eyes, which sharply differentiated me from the olive-skinned, dark-eyed Italian women that drew attention to me.

For a couple of years after this trip, I dallied with the idea of one day applying for another, post-graduate Erasmus scholarship to study art in Florence. I could amble about the streets at my own leisurely pace, going nowhere in particular, usually alone but sometimes accompanied by a dashing Florentine man. Perhaps it would be in Italy where I might discover the true nature of romantic passion, to be cooled down afterwards with a tutti-frutti gelato.

13

Appreciating One's Good Fortune by Giving Succour to Convicts

And so the day rolled round when I returned to England. I was sad to leave Amsterdam behind but brought a little bit of it over on the ferry with me in the form of an old bicycle with its leather saddle bags filled with my favourite Dutch junk food.

My summer job, where the student workers were provided by the same charitable organisation I'd worked for last summer, was with Her Majesty's Probation Services. The semi-open detention centre was for women with young children who were awaiting trial. I'd live in a flat upstairs with Maggie, the other student working there through her summer holiday, and we'd just be 'helpers'. It was a vague job description but I gradually understood the basic expectations. There was also a rotation of qualified probation officers both during the day and overnight so that there'd never be too much pressure on Maggie and me. Maggie was seriously considering a career in the probation service but I wasn't. I still had no specific career in mind, but I did feel that I made a bit of a difference in that place.

The crimes of the women who lived there ranged from the macabre to the ridiculous, from manslaughter to horse rustling, but they were all free to come and go during the day, taking their children to school, going shopping and such like. Maria, an outgoing and affable mother of three who was awaiting trial for killing her abusive husband in self defence, had lived in one room with her children for over a year due to delays by the Crown Prosecution Service. Amy, the horse rustler, was an unworldly seventeen-year-old whose boyfriend had wanted to give her a horse because he believed it was every girl's dream. He'd found one nearby that was easy to steal, which he'd then moved to a disused field near Amy's house. She admitted that she'd known what he was doing and had been accused of being an accomplice. She was now heavily pregnant with his child and awaiting her hearing.

The other residents all hated nineteen-year-old Kirsty whom they referred to as 'The Muppet'. Even though Kirsty was alarmingly simple, she had, nevertheless, gone along with her boyfriend in the heinous robbery of an old lady which had involved violence of a torture-like nature, with her as a spaced-out onlooker. For me, she epitomized the expression 'mooncalf', with her vacant saucer eyes in an expressionless face, behind which there was little in the way of thought. It was hard for me to chat with her knowing the nature of the crime to which she had been party, particularly with my feelings for my grandmothers, but she had a newborn baby whom she wasn't caring for properly so we all had to pitch in. The expectation was that she'd receive a prison sentence and the baby would be adopted, but first she was going to have her trial.

I noticed that whenever the probation officers went to see Kirsty, they scowled at her, focusing on her lack of care for her baby and exhibiting a 'shame on you' attitude. She would sit with her arms folded, grumpy in the corner and leave the room, slamming the door, when the baby cried. I decided to experiment with some reverse psychology to try to address this issue: I'd ignore the baby when I went to see Kirsty and just sit and chat with her.

There was a transformation after three visits to Kirsty's room. She suddenly asked me why I never showed any interest in the baby. In an attempt to pique my interest, she pointed out the nice dress she'd put on her and how well she was drinking from her bottle. Professing my genuine ignorance about babies, I asked her to show me how to bathe a baby and what was the best way to hold one. We soon started going on walks to the park and the shops with the baby in her pram. Kirsty felt acknowledged and brightened up, showing a sound level of care for the baby, who stopped crying so much because she was no longer being neglected.

The staff were amazed at the progress, but it surprised me that, despite their being seasoned professionals in their field of social work, it had taken an inexperienced student to see that Kirsty was a traumatized child herself, one who needed care and attention, and that once this happened she would, hopefully, become capable of giving care and attention. After I left, I was told Kirsty was eventually sent to prison and the baby was adopted. At least, I thought, she would be able to remember that she'd been a decent mother for a time.

Another resident I felt I helped was Arleen, a Jamaican lady in her thirties who was fiercely defensive of anyone approaching her toddler, Ruby. She had alienated most of the other residents because of this. I asked one of the probation officers what this was about and she told me Arleen's sad story. Arleen had been selling drugs and was on the run from the police with her young son and Ruby, at that time a small baby. Her son had died during the chase. Of course, she felt responsible and I could understand why she never smiled. His ashes were in her room wrapped in the Jamaican flag. Even though they were very different people, I adopted a similar approach to the one I had with Kirsty, in that whenever I went to see Arleen, I'd ignore Ruby. Eventually, Ruby had toddled over to me and put her hands on my knees and Arleen had allowed it without a trace of being defensive.

Arleen was restless because she was confined to the grounds as there was some suspicion that she might jump probation so I taught her tennis on the court around the back of the building. She would take along Ruby who'd sit at the side in a little playpen with her toys. We went every morning for the three months I was there. Very soon, Arleen was better at tennis than I was and scolding me for not trying harder.

One of the saddest revelations to me while working at that place was that most of the women there were survivors of incest. On learning this, I suddenly felt grateful for my childhood which, although difficult towards the end, was nothing compared to what all of these women had been through.

Maggie and I would occasionally visit Azra, a former resident of Bangladeshi background, who'd been exonerated from a charge of murder and was now living in her own flat in a secret location. She had been abused by numerous family members, which had led to a pregnancy. Some of the uncles, attempting to conceal their crime, had killed her baby girl and, when the district midwife had discovered the baby was missing, the uncles had tried to blame it on Azra. Azra was amiable with a reserved smile and a gentle manner. On one of our visits, she told us that it would have been her daughter's third birthday on that day.

When I had time off, I sometimes felt the need to go on a day trip to put a physical distance between myself and my workplace so I could forget the sorrows of the residents for a while. I would go over to Stratford-upon-Avon on the little local train to see the plays by the RSC, with their depiction of the full Shakespearean spectrum of human grandeur and depravity. As a result of this, along with my fine experiences of acting thus far, a stronger notion than at Wyndham took shape in my mind to pursue an acting career. Of course, I was, as yet, ignorant of the scale of effort involved in achieving the scantest of livings as an actor.

14

Departing this World

As my summer job came to an end, May died. I returned to Whitehaven and, on the day of the funeral, walked along Hilltop Road to St Peter's church with Manda, the cold wind whipping around us despite it only being September. Manda's hat was blown off her head and we had to chase it up the road, or rather I did as she was no longer up to hat chasing. We laughed at her brief attempt to join in but beneath my smile I was preoccupied by concern that Manda's funeral was probably not so far off either.

May's coffin, in a pale wood, was parked on a chrome trolley at the front of the church. I was taken aback by how small it was, and how much old age had diminished her. She'd been such a formidable presence around whom I'd so often tip-toed, and here was an almost child-sized coffin. Seeing this filled me with a deep sorrow, but not one that could be released with tears, so tearless I remained. I was wearing the blue embroidered blouse she had liked so much when I'd shown it to her a couple of years before.

The vicar gave a brief, generic sermon and my

Uncle Derek let out a sudden sob, the most emotional I'd seen him. He was a stoic man who'd been an ambulance driver for most of his working life so he was accustomed to death and injury. We all sang 'Abide With Me' and, even though May had not been religious, I wished it could have been a less feeble rendition for her sake. Being his usual antisocial self, Jim begrudgingly perched on the end of our pew at the front, with a substantial space between him and his brother. He dashed off at the end, refusing my mother's invitation for us to have lunch together in the local pub.

In May's will, she had stated which piece of her jewelry she wanted each of her granddaughters to have but it was no longer possible to carry out her instructions because, during the time she'd been in the old folks' home, Jim had rummaged through her possessions and sold off whatever he could. Of course, he denied this but it was the only explanation for the disappearances as only he was in the house. I felt cross that his sense of entitlement reduced him to having no care for his mother and that he had only seen her as someone he could extract from: free housing, free coal, free food and plundering her personal effects when she was infirm, robbing her of her last wishes.

May's beloved grandfather clock, which she had wound every night, was wrecked in her absence because he stuck in a modern, battery powered mechanism, damaging it beyond repair due to his being annoyed at having to wind it. He had also, behind his siblings' backs, arranged the sale of the house to one of his acquaintances for a dishonorably low price. It was probable that he'd received a wad of cash under the table for the favour. When the sale was finalised, he'd moved out, clearing a little living space in the crammed bungalow he'd built.

What upset my mother most, however, was Jim's conduct at May's deathbed in the West Cumberland Hospital, the place where most of Whitehaven's residents go to die. They had been called to the hospital as May was fading. My mother was sitting beside her holding her hand, while Jim, of course, was sullenly hanging back. Just as May breathed her last, Jim announced to the nurse, 'Well, we'd better get on with arranging the funeral then'. My mother had read that those pronounced dead may still be aware of their surroundings in the minutes after their breathing stops and she was distraught to think this was the last thing her mother might've heard. Jim's sudden death would come a year later almost to the day and in the same room at the same hospital. My mother went to his bedside too, and even shed a tear when her selfish brother breathed his last.

In Jim's will, he left everything to Mary, a spinster he'd befriended in later life, who was supported in style by a wealthy brother who worked abroad so she had no need of his bequest. Jim may have entertained the idea that Mary would want to live in his bungalow, as if she were the spouse he never had. After all, it would have been his marital home, had he married Cora. But Mary didn't want to live there. She immediately sent around estate agents to assess it who said it was unsellable in its current condition so she gave my mother and Derek a key and told them they could have what was inside, not out of generosity, but rather as a means of clearing the place before it went on the market.

My mother and Derek saw that, apart from the little area he'd cleared for his bed, the bungalow was full to the brim with unusual items with which to furnish a home. There was a large circular saw in the sitting room surrounded by piles of timber. In the kitchen, numerous engine parts were balanced on the work surfaces. Under Jim's bed were boxes of tools, along with a cardboard box of the hardback books about mining from the parlour and squashed at the bottom of this *A Young Lady's Miscellany*, which I asked my mother to save for me should she come across it. When they opened up the garage, they were surprised to discover beneath tarpaulins a substantial motor yacht Jim had built from scratch over the decades, beautifully crafted and in a nearly finished state. Not being seagoing types themselves, my mother and Derek, sold the boat for a tidy sum, which would, no doubt, have had Jim grumbling in his grave.

While I was in Whitehaven for May's funeral, I visited Michael Moon's bookshop, not because I wanted anything in particular, but because it was just one of the pilgrimages I tended to make whenever I was home. I removed an interesting-looking illustrated version of Robert Burton's *Anatomy of Melancholy* from a shelf only to discover a copper-coloured eye looking at me through the hole where the book had been. 'I'm spying on you,' the eye said. I hurriedly replaced the book and peered around the bookcase. There stood my old flame, Marcus, in his yellow waistcoat grinning maniacally, his unusually sharp canines on display.

'Did you get another boyfriend?' he burst out, 'I did. Girlfriend, I mean. She's called Poppy. She's much prettier than you and cleverer too.'

'I'm so pleased to hear it, Marcus,' I replied, 'But if you don't mind, I'm here for my grandmother's funeral and not really in the mood for idle chit-chat.'

'Oh, I'm so sorry,' he babbled, 'Shall we go to the grave together?'

'That sounds like an attempt to rekindle a tragic romance that was never kindled to begin with,' I said but he wasn't listening.

'I...I mean your grandmother's grave. We like graveyards, don't we, the two of us? Majestic places. I saw a badger up there once.'

It was hard to shake him off and finally I went into Woolworth's because I knew he wouldn't follow me in there as he detested the place, considering it to be 'common'. I hid behind the pick-and-mix and waited until he drifted off.

I noticed on this visit that Whitehaven had been smartened up a little, courtesy of the local nuclear power station's largesse. There were some stylish new iron benches, cycle racks with a fish theme and decorative cobblestone mosaics depicting mermaids in the pedestrian areas. In 1957, Britain's worst nuclear accident had occurred at this power station and, throughout the following decades, gestures were made here and there, possibly as a form of danger money thinly veiled as corporate public relations. The harbour had also been improved in that a retaining wall had been built which prevented all the water going out at low tide so the boats didn't have to sit in stinking, unsightly mud half the time.

The trenchcoated old fellows with their grey-hounds were no longer wandering the deserted streets, seemingly replaced by more well-heeled retirees. The estate agents had ramped up the price of property significantly, claiming that Whitehaven was the 'Gateway to the Lake District', despite its being a forty minute drive to the nearest lake.

I didn't see Roger, my mother's long-term para-mour on this trip as he had left her for a younger woman with a bungalow in landscaped grounds. My mother had briefly experimented with lonely hearts columns but she'd not been thrilled with the one date she'd had so far. Selecting a service station, as it was on neutral territory, they had met in the cafe but when he walked in, he had been 'lame', she told me, which 'he'd not mentioned prior to the meeting'.

On my way back to college that September, I stopped off to see Elspeth at her beloved farm. I had envisaged her home as a quaint cobbled farmyard dotted with chickens and piebald cows meandering in from the fields to the thatched milking shed. Elspeth had learned to drive so she collected me from the train station in her father's ancient Austin Allegro. We drove along narrow lanes with tall hedgerows, rabbits nibbling at the undergrowth.

'Here we are!' Elspeth announced.

I was confused because it didn't look at all how I'd imagined it. The farmhouse was a couple of 1960s red brick semi-detached houses, not a pretty cottage trimmed with honeysuckle, whilst the farmyard was cracked concrete, instead of cobbles. We drove past a fenced structure with a corrugated asbestos roof where cattle stood shoulder to shoulder, caked in their own dirt.

'Don't your cows live in a field?' I asked, hopefully.

'Ooo no, that'd be too much work for Dadda nowadays. They just stay in the barn and the milking shed is right next door.'

I concluded that I'd been harbouring a few too many clichéd preconceptions about contemporary farming, as with the 'vicarage' in Birmingham the previous year. Inside the farmhouse, the broken illusion continued with no sign of an Aga, just a modern gas oven and laminated chipboard kitchen units, although the family did indeed take milk directly from the teat via a galvanized jug, shunning the pasteurized stuff that couldn't give you salmonella. This was fair enough, but when we first walked across the yard, Elspeth had pointed out a cow who had mastitis and was due to be collected by the slaughterhouse. I chose toast instead of cornflakes with milk for my breakfast the next morning. For the first time, I pondered the possibility that vegans, whom I'd always considered extremists who took animal welfare too far, might just be in the right that dairy farming, at least as practiced on a commercial scale, was only marginally less cruel than beef rearing.

15

Thespian Aspirations Dashed

Two days later, I was pleased to continue with my journey back to college for my final year as I was thoroughly ready to get away from the dung redolent air. Elspeth and I travelled back by train. We'd be living in the centre of town together, along with Jenny and Claire. There was still going to be something of an atmosphere of a girls' wing but at least it would be in a pleasant Georgian townhouse, rather than along a linoleum floored corridor.

Elspeth still evinced no interest in partaking of pleasures of the flesh until she blushed to her ginger roots, giving us all a hint of her deeper psyche when, one evening, a man came to the door. The doorbell rang and Elspeth answered it. From the kitchen, we were surprised to hear a masculine voice say something about a 'cock'. Upon the utterance of that syllable, the rest of us naturally hastened to the door, where Elspeth was floundering, clearly overwhelmed. Paul, everyone's favourite lecturer, was standing there like Lady Chatterley's gamekeeper, pulling a headless fowl from a hessian sack. He proceeded to explain that he'd finally had to decapitate his cockerel with an axe due to his neighbours' complaints about the perpetual racket it raised at daybreak. He was now offering his rooster to us impoverished young lady students. Elspeth swiftly accepted, plucked her prize and ate it up all by herself with a look of faraway ecstasy in her eyes, probably the closest she'd ever get, so we joked behind her back, to having a cock inside her.

Meanwhile, I continued with my vegetarian cookery in our well-equipped kitchen. Some of the more experimental efforts went awry, however, such as when I made leaden buckwheat pancakes that even the birds wouldn't touch when I flung them out onto the front lawn where they languished through the winter. 'Have you still not mastered pancakes?!' the incredulous voice of Mrs. Shackleton scolded me inside my head. I tried to make excuses regarding the extra challenge presented by buckwheat flour and she suggested I stick to the more conventional recipe in future.

I received a postcard from my father informing me he was visiting old pals in nearby Selby and was planning to drive over to meet me in a certain pub he was acquainted with. I hadn't seen him for a couple of years and his offer to meet up surprised me. I invited Jenny to come along as we'd frequently compared notes on the contrasting attributes of our disagreeable fathers. We were expecting a cheap ploughman's lunch, at the very least but he only offered us a glass of lemonade and instructed the bartender to put two straws in it. As he sucked on his pint, he told me he'd been sacked and couldn't find another job so now he was broke. Morose and self-absorbed, he made an even less favourable impression on Jenny than she'd anticipated, based on what I'd told her about him. By the end of the pub visit, I was almost expecting him to ask me for a handout, or try to cadge our couch for the night. He didn't ask about how I was doing, no enquiries about my literature course, or how my time in Amsterdam had been or how I was managing financially. There was no interest. It was only me asking questions and adding kind responses to his cheerless monologue.

When we parted, I was relieved but the meeting left me miserable for a few days. The last thing he said was that he was going to ask a friend in India if there were any managerial jobs he could get in Mumbai. I later found out that he had done something—neither of my sisters was quite sure what— in his last job in Stoke-on-Trent that was going to make it very difficult for him to get an executive job in Britain again, hence his plans to go very far away.

He wrote me a postcard from Mumbai a few months later, saying he was in charge of the construction of a new factory and what a pleasure it was to deal with workers who were 'happy' to be paid, not with money but with a daily dish of rice and lentils for ten hours of unskilled labouring in excavation or construction. After a few more years, he blotted his copybook on the international executive head-hunting circuit as well and headed off to Bangkok where he utilized his international savings to invest in a group of three laundrettes, as part of which business deal, he also obtained the services of a younger, Thai business partner who became the day-to-day manageress and, briefly, his girlfriend.

During these latter years of his high-flying career, he liked to pop back to Whitehaven every summer where he would gad about doused in aftershave, wearing a powder-blue sports jacket, patent leather shoes and a white open necked shirt which revealed a glint of a gold chain around his neck. Rumour had it, more than likely initiated by himself, that he 'lived off his interest'.

I asked Paul, the poet, to direct me and a couple of friends in a Pinter three-hander called *Old Times*, in which a man tries to remember his relationships with two women who are muddled up in his mind. This was pertinent for me at that time, in the wake of my own anticlimactic and puzzling first 'proper' boyfriend, Jan the pianist, who had as little to say to me as I did to him once we parted company in Amsterdam. On a roll following the success of the Pinter play—which was so good that we made a mini tour of other regional college campuses—Paul directed me and a larger circle of acquaintances in Chekhov's *The Three Sisters*.

I decided to have another go at having a boy-friend. Carl was another actor in the play, fair haired and slightly built, like Jan, albeit shorter and, lo and behold, another disappointment in my nether regions. I wondered if there might be a prob-lem with me physically, because I'd received more gratification from zooming over speed bumps on my antiquated Dutch bicycle.

In a cagey manner, I leafed through the women's magazines in WH Smiths which were running articles on the mysterious 'O'. I imagined these periodicals being hawked on the streets by the crusty old newspaper vendors of the past, 'Find your pinnacle of passion here, ladies! Read all about it!'. I experimented with some of the tactics recommended with Carl but it continued to be a blink-or-you'll-miss-it scenario. He was a sweet boy, nevertheless, always apologetic. He'd come from a family situation next to which my own paled. His mother had died when he was small and his uninterested father had married one of those evil stepmother types that I too had been briefly acquainted with, only his experience lasted for years. She'd rationed his food, which became particularly difficult when Carl was a growing teenager so he'd had to smuggle muesli out of the kitchen in a mug pretending it was a cup of tea.

He was inordinately nice to me, bringing me chocolate when I had the monthly cramps and writing songs about me on his guitar. Due to his being anxious about performing, onstage and otherwise, he sang from his neck up, which resulted in his voice sounding nasal and strangled, but I thanked him for the songs all the same. His guitar playing was accomplished because he was constantly tinkering with the instrument in an obsessive compulsive way, which irritated me at first, although I was able to not notice after a while, and forgave him once I realised he'd taken up guitar as a comfort in his lonely boyhood.

He liked to do Tai Chi Chuan in parks wearing special Chinese slippers and a baggy Tai Chi suit, which influenced his general clothing style. These Tai Chi sessions could go on for over an hour but they so transfixed him that he wasn't aware if I nipped off back to my house for tea and biscuits.

Given the gender demographic of my college, with its scarcity of males, I allowed the liaison to linger.

During this final year at university, I resolved to apply for an acting course at one of the famous drama schools in London. It was a major expense for me with the train fare and even an audition fee. On arrival, I was handed a badge with my name and under it, the words *Musical Theatre*.

'Why is Musical Theatre written on my badge?' I enquired, confused.

'Because that's what you applied for, dear,' the receptionist told me and showed me my application form, where indeed I had, in error, ticked Musical Theatre.

'Can't I change to the plain acting audition?' I pleaded.

'We're auditioning for that next week and it's full. We could put you on the reserve list but you'll have to pay the audition fee again.'

I couldn't afford another train fare let alone another audition fee, and did not wish to be hauled before the bank manager again, so I decided to give it a go, whatever exactly it was. The only musical theatre I'd seen was the 'Tits, tits, I wish I had tits!' show when I was a child so I really didn't have a clue.

Before I knew it, I was whisked along, handed a page of words and asked to sing. I didn't really know how to sing along with a pianist, as in when I was supposed to join in with her playing so, after a couple of false starts, she gave me a big nod and off I went. I actually sang fairly adequately, standing next to an upright piano in a room full of staring people with four judges sitting behind a table looking tired.

The person after me introduced herself as what sounded like 'Mere Calories', which was ironic as she was stout. I imagined her saying her name and laughing as she tossed morsels of cake into her mouth and felt an immediate affinity with her. It soon became apparent that Mere Calories was a trained opera singer as she blew the ceiling off the room and woke up the judges with a start. I could see my offering in the singing heats fading to obscurity.

Next up was the hour-long dance audition, a farcical experience for me. I was always considered somewhat bold in my freestyle dancing, but when asked to follow prescribed steps, I was dancelexic. Mere Calories was a superb dancer, throwing every ounce of her ample flesh into the groove. The girl next to me had been at the Royal Ballet's White Lodge since infancy and positively sailed through. I was in the wilting minority, having never had a dance lesson before and being attired in not a thread of professional dancewear. When the time finally came to perform our prepared dramatic monologues, I was worn out and certain it no longer mattered anyway.

Out of the room of twenty hopefuls at the audition that day, most of whom were highly competent at singing and dancing, only two were asked to remain to go onto the next round, the Royal Ballet girl and Mere Calories. Adding up the fees collected from our group, I realised that audition season was a highly lucrative endeavor for these institutions and, feeling more than a bit of a fool, tossed my badge into the bin on my way out.

When I returned to college, I hurriedly called around a dozen or so acting courses only to find that either they were full or required an additional skill like miming, or fencing, or playing a musical instrument. All I had were my sketchy skills on the recorder so I decided not to bother. By only signing up for one audition, I'd put all my eggs in one thespian basket with the naive notion that they'd definitely accept me.

Each week I bought a copy of *The Stage* and duly scoured the casting calls. These were primarily for 'Go-Go Dancers' but in spite of having a chest that was ideal for this calling, I felt that it was out of my remit, following the disastrous dance auditions in which I'd failed so epically. The real acting jobs were few and far between and all required something called an Equity Card, which I soon discovered you couldn't get until you'd done dozens of hours of professional acting work. It was an archetypal catch-twenty-two situation and I had no clue how to get around it. I left college after receiving my very good, yet at the same time essentially worthless, degree from the robotic, white-gloved hand of the Duchess of Kent, without any plan for the future.

16

Initiation into the Mystery Cycle

I viewed a succession of depressing little rooms in shared houses in York. One of these was entirely inhabited by older men who all looked like they were one step away from homelessness. At the time of my visit, they were communally frying onions and tomatoes in the shared kitchen to have with some sausages. I finally settled upon a large ground floor bedsit in the centre of York, which had a concealed kitchenette behind wobbly wooden cabinetry. There was a shared bathroom out in the hallway with a voluminous cast iron bathtub. My bedsit had once been the fine parlour of a smart Georgian town house so there was the obligatory showy marble fireplace and two tall sash windows. As there was no heating, I would turn on my oven and open the door to warm up the room to save me buying a heater. The whole building was down at heel, and badly maintained but that was good for me as it meant the rent was low.

After going into hospital to have all four of my wisdom teeth removed because they were coming in sideways, I accepted some temporary work at the dole office. This proved to be a demonstration of my new dental state in that it was a move wholly lacking in wisdom. The job, if one could call it that, consisted of sitting for days on end, alone in a basement room lined with filing cabinets, shredding any client's paperwork which had 'deceased' stamped on the front. In spite of shredding constantly, I made barely a dent in their congested records. Feeling more and more deceased and shredded myself, I decided to supplant my post with something above ground that would situate me slightly more in the land of the living. I got a job as a waitress in a cosy and informal restaurant in the city centre.

I'd struggled to get all my school qualifications, worked hard to get a good degree only to end up in a job for which, ironically, I needed no qualifications other than a tidy appearance and a pleasant manner. Still, I was probably in a better position than Tim who, for the Christmas holidays, could find nothing better than a job as Santa in a supermarket in Leeds, where he was repeatedly kicked in the shins by disaffected brats.

Although tired out by eight hour waitressing shifts, there was a decent wage plus a share of the generous tips at the end of the night, which meant I was better off than I'd been as a shredder in Her Majesty's civil service. I hadn't seen or heard from Carl for a few months, although I did have one of his many guitars in my wardrobe, which he'd needed someone to look after over the summer. I wondered whether this favour had been engineered as an excuse to visit me. When I wasn't working, I would often stare into the wooded grounds of the fee-paying school opposite watching the pupils doing military drills with mock rifles. Such was the strange world of education for the privileged.

I hadn't entirely given up on the idea of acting some day and was excited to see an advert for auditions for dozens of parts in *The York Mystery Plays*, a cycle of Biblical dramatic sketches written down in Medieval times, which focused upon the key episodes in the history of the cosmos according to Christian doctrine. It was normally performed in the city park every four years with the ruins of the city's main monastery as a backdrop. Due to interruptions of past performances owing to bad weather, York City Council had, this time, moved it into the gold leaf trimmed, flouncy curtained York Theatre Royal, which was hardly a fitting setting for a rough and tumble cycle of Medieval drama. I couldn't complain though because there was no need for the elusive Equity Card and anyone could take part.

The York Mystery Plays had been Judi Dench's springboard into acting back in the late 1950s after she'd been cast as the Virgin Mary. I knew a lot had changed in the acting world in the thirty-odd years since her lucky break but I thought I'd have a go anyway and, after a handful of auditions, was given the part of Eve.

Initially, I was jubilant that I'd been offered one of the main parts. However, following some chuckled reactions when I told people about my big break, it dawned on me that I might well be asked to play my part wearing a fig leaf at the most, and that this may have been a prime consideration in choosing me for the role. Was I to have my day as a go-go dancer, after all, only in an idiosyncratic Medieval context?

As was the tradition in York's Mystery Plays, a professional actor was chosen for the main role of Christ. This time round, however, the choice wasn't exactly impressive because the actor selected was a regular in a television series as popular as it was mediocre. The other members of the cast were non-professionals, although some of them were hoping, far more assuredly than I, that this would be their entry ticket to a professional career as ours was to be a high profile production.

The actor playing Satan, undoubtedly the most interesting role in the play, looked perfect for the part, being tall and lean with a full head of curls and piercing blue eyes. In another league from the rest of us, his dramatic skills outshone everyone else's by far, including those of the semi-famous television actor playing Christ, who was, fittingly enough, a little cagey around Satan.

A gaggle of ambitious young actors orbited syco-phantically around the semi-famous television actor, clearly hopeful that he might give them a leg-up in their future careers with an introduction to a casting director. They'd bring him a coffee, run errands for him and laugh too hard at his jokes. This flunkeyism made me cringe and, joining the ranks of Satan, I refused to participate in it. One of this bunch did receive the favour he was aiming for and ultimately became far more successful than the semi-famous television actor himself, reinforcing the lesson that in acting, much like its half-sibling politics, fawning can sometimes take you far.

I had an appointment to be measured for my cos-tume, which was a relief as this indicated I wasn't going to be naked on stage. The director of the play, a living caricature of the foibles of his profession, had decided on a contemporary approach and Adam and Eve would be wearing silver lycra body suits that would cling to every crevice so I resolved to start doing sit-ups.

I wasn't really into the director's 'vision' of setting the play in a building site with scaffolding which, someone suggested, was just a rip-off of the original productions of *Godspell* and *Jesus Christ Superstar*. It was, however, pointless to disagree with the fellow as I learnt to my cost when I tried out a different approach to a line from the one dictated to me. A 'Get back in your box' response, that put me in mind of my father, was instantly dispatched. As the director was fond of telling us, he had thirty years of experience at the finest regional theatres in England under his belt so he knew best. Being treated as a marionette in my little 'taster' of professional acting was a sobering disappointment.

In the Medieval era, these plays were performed by regular working people. That tradition had been continued with all the parts played by residents of York leading ordinary lives, with the exception of the crowd-pulling professional actor. In our production, Satan was a teacher, God was a bank teller, The Virgin Mary worked in a bookshop, I was a waitress. The chance to be in this production was meant to offer everyday folk an out-of-the-ordinary experience and I could see that, for some, this was a bit too much to cope with and made them go a tad awry.

Perhaps it was something about stepping out of a quotidian existence and assuming another identity but I could see the uptightness being peeled away in the warm-up sessions. The cast began calling one another 'darling' and engaging in things like luvvie hugs and kisses on both cheeks which gradually slipped into bottom smacks. Extramarital affairs soon started taking place up in the derelict dressing rooms at the top of the old theatre. The participants would return to the rehearsal room with the tell-tale signs of plaster dust and cobwebs on their clothes. Naturally, Mary Magdalene, an attractive divorcee in her forties, was an obvious point of interest but she sensibly turned down any offers.

Surprisingly, it was the pale, bookish, rather awkward girl playing the Virgin Mary who was most often besmirched with plaster dust and cobwebs. During a cast party held half way through the rehearsal period, she became very friendly indeed with one of the angels, a fireman who was married with a young family during the day. I too was guilty of joining in somewhat with the theatrical louche-ness at this particular party, where alcohol flowed copiously. I had a one night stand with a divorced man fifteen years older than me, whom I thought might bring the benefit of experience to bedding me, but who turned out to be yet another dull-as-dishwater unerotic experience. Earlier in the evening, he'd told me that of all the people who'd ever taken a shine to him, I'd been the only one born after England had won the World Cup. Continuing on this football theme back at his house, the manner in which he cheered as he metaphorically dribbled his ball through the goal posts reminded me of a lout in a pub watching his favourite team. As I lay back and thought of England winning the Cup, I continued to wonder about the point of it all other than for procreation.

And that was where Jay came in. I was often upstairs in the reading room of York library because it was warmer than my bedsit. I liked to read a book or a newspaper or write a short story because I'd started going to an evening class where we read our work aloud and then had discussions. I suddenly noticed a pair of intense greyish green eyes regarding me through round tortoise-shell glasses at the slanted reading table opposite mine. His shoulder-length brown hair was tied back with an elastic band and he wore a tweed herring-bone jacket and a tie depicting mallards in flight.

'Is your name Rebecca?' he asked in an accent I couldn't quite place, 'Have we met before?'

I shook my head quickly and carried on with my story.

'What are you writing about?'

I stared back at him in wonder. You weren't supposed to speak in the reading room and, in any case, I was hesitant about sharing my writing outside my evening class.

'I can't tell you,' I whispered.

'Oh, why not?' he enquired, as if he were some psychotherapist, but with the eye of an overly curious parrot.

'Because I don't want to!' I hissed, my voice becoming louder which resulted in me being shush-ed by the librarian.

'Do you want to go with me to Choose a Cheese, the shop in the Shambles? They have superlative cheddar and they give free samples,' he asked, standing up.

I didn't know how to respond to this cheese-date proposition so looked down and carried on with my writing, puzzled by his forwardness.

I saw him again a few days later at a Saturday night performance at York Arts Centre where I volunteered in the ticket booth in return for getting free admission to the plays. I sold him a ticket and said hello. He was with a woman with a wide face like a tomcat, a loose ginger afro and a silk mini-dress. As he sat in the auditorium, I noticed he was watching me more than the performance. The woman, on the other hand, was watching him more than the play and looking disheartened. After the performance, I asked him where his friend was and he told me she had gone home to her son.

Outside the silent zone of the reading room, I was more amenable to answering his slew of questions and to asking some of my own. He was from New York and had ended up in Old York after an argument with his then-girlfriend who'd literally kicked him out of her car. Thinking York looked okay, he'd decided to settle there for the time being. He'd rented a room and got himself a job writing pamphlets at a small public relations and advertising agency, the eccentric owner of which liked to ride into work on a horse. He'd just finished editing a pamphlet on the stained glass in York Minster's Rose Window and was about to launch what he described as 'a major campaign for a revolutionary new kind of dog harness', which he proceeded to explain to me in detail. He appeared to be in possession of a brain teeming with information, more than any other brain I'd encountered, anyway.

We discovered that we lived very near each other and began to walk home together. Micklegate, where the Arts Centre was situated, was already thronging with Saturday night people. The males all dressed alike, as did the females, as if they were in uniform for a night school where sex was the only subject. The men, barely out of boyhood, were all in fitted jeans belted with a prominent chunky metal buckle, plainly intended to draw attention to the package on offer just below. They usually wore half-unbuttoned white shirts above and so much gel in their hair that it looked wet. The women, some of them possibly not yet out of girlhood, all sported very short dresses and, if there were any knickers beneath at all, they were nothing like the sensible ones Manda used to hang out on her washing line. Some of the dresses looked like the shirts the boys were wearing, only the big belt was cinched tighter and higher on the waist and it looked as if they'd forgotten to put their trousers on before they went out. Teetering in their heels, they made a beeline to the pubs and clubs up the hill in an all girl group while the boys ascended in their boy group across the road. A couple of hours later they would all descend, now in a mixed group, whooping and snogging, but with some of them irate because their one night stands hadn't panned out favourably. I was glad we'd encountered them heading up the hill sober, rather than on the drunken downward procession later.

A few days after this, Jay appeared at my humble abode, knocking on the window and pointing at a bag of shopping that turned out to be ingredients for a Chinese meal. He created an excellent concoction in my shabby little kitchenette, probably inching toward my heart via way of my stomach. I was surprised to see him bash the garlic with a jar to make the skin fall off, but decided I must adopt the practice myself in future. I asked about the woman he'd been with at the play and he explained things had been difficult with her because when they had attempted to become intimate, she had caused him to come out in a rash, the same way he did when he interacted with cats.

Jay's room in a house around the corner was sublet to him by a single father with teenage children who had such an aversion to work that he had successfully negotiated the benefits system for a couple of decades, sometimes whilst also earning cash on the side as a gardener. Occasionally, this man, who had certain 'high' expenses, would run out of money to pay the bills so that their gas, water or electric would be cut off. A few times after this occurred, Jay turned up at my bedsit asking to use the large bathtub in the shared bathroom, which also happened to have an ample hot water supply, so that he could go to his office in a clean condition.

We started taking occasional strolls on the riverside path where he would talk and talk. He told me he'd been such a chatterbox as a boy that in middle school, after having been warned again and again to 'shut the hell up' by some of his more athletic classmates, they had locked him into one of those tall lockers that always seem to line the corridors of American schools in films for a few hours to teach him a lesson. It had worked, he reported, but only temporarily.

One day, Carl unexpectedly appeared on my door-step asking for his guitar back. Cordially, I invited him in. He saw a note I'd stuck on my door a few days ago and forgotten to take down, telling Jay I might be late for a walk we'd arranged, and that he should 'hang on a minute'. Carl questioned me sus-piciously, despite my not having seen him for so long, at which point I instantly regretted never hav-ing formally broken things off with him, expecting he would just take the hint. I told him about my new friend, for that was all Jay was, and offered to make lunch for him. When I smashed the garlic with a jar, he looked at me in wonder and I explained this was a trick I'd learned from Jay. 'That's an awfully brash, American sort of thing to do!' Carl chided. He wolfed down the meal I prepared, despite his disapproval of my unorthodox garlic peeling method, took his guitar and left in a mood. I never saw him again.

On the first night of *The Mystery Plays*, there'd been a technical hitch in the semi-famous television actor's crucifixion scene, during which he'd filled in the down time by coming out of character and bantering with the audience from the cross. I'd been mortified by this unintended homage to Monty Python's *The Life of Brian*. Regrettably, a few reviewers for national papers had seen the play on opening night and mentioned the professional's unprofessionalism. *The Stage* had also reviewed the play and I'd been mentioned with an accolade, which I thought just might be my golden ticket into the elusive thespian domain.

I sent off a handful of impassioned letters each day for a few weeks to every theatre company in the country, accompanied by the mandatory black and white headshot, which I'd developed and printed myself at minimal cost in the Arts Centre dark room. Not one wrote back. It didn't help that, around this time on a walk with Jay, I peered through the windows of an abandoned casting agency business in a little building down by the River Ouse, where we saw heaps of professionally done headshots left strewn all over the floor. I was becoming more and more unsure about pushing myself to the fore in a field chock-full of starry-eyed hopefuls willing to do whatever it took to get on therein.

Meanwhile, Judas Iscariot had invited me to his house for his birthday with a few other members of the cast including the semi-famous television actor. Cycling there, I passed Jay and brought him along perched on my rear rack. After the nice Happy Birthday singing and excellent chocolate cake, someone presented Judas with a massive spliff in a gift-wrapped box. Naturally, this was not featured in the Renaissance paintings of Judas on Jesus's left side. We then sat round in the traditional circle to partake of it by candlelight. Remembering the unfortunate episode in Amsterdam on my bicycle after hash brownies, I reluctantly had a couple of quick puffs. By the time it was coming round to me a third time, I had turned green in the smoke-filled room so excused myself. I spent the next half hour in the host's bathroom in a condition similar to what had befallen me whenever I'd make the mistake of eating chocolate, or cherries, or Angel Delight, or numerous other things as a child. Jay came in and helped me through the worst of it in a most gentlemanly manner—as if he were thoroughly accustomed to witnessing all his young lady friends with their heads over the toilet—before cycling me back to my bedsit, this time with me perched on the rack.

The play ran through July for twenty-five performances. Saturdays were hard going because there was a matinee as well as an evening performance. *The York Mystery Plays* are infamous for their length of over four hours, which, combined with the Middle English dialect in which they were written, can be quite a challenge for an audience. It was, therefore, fortunate that my Adam and Eve scene came near the start when the audience weren't yet flagging.

For me, after the first week, it all started dragging and I started to feel bored with the lines I'd had in my head for a few months now. The director was against experimentation and spontaneity so no one was to alter their scenes during the performance, even if suddenly struck by a great idea. It was to be acted exactly the same every night, which made it appear stale. Continuing to feel like a marionette, I developed further reservations about my suitability for the acting profession, finding it at once tiresome and draining to play the same scenes again and again with authenticity. The tedious *Jesus Christ Superstar* and *Godspell* imitating contemporary production had, as I had feared all along, turned out to be dull. We could see it in the audience's faces, around five hundred of them for every performance and with a goodly number clearly dropping off to sleep before us.

I tried to persuade a girl in the bit part of 'a tormented soul', who was having similar problems to me in getting any auditions, to have done with it and do a teaching certificate which I'd just found out about. 'It's really easy to get on one of these courses,' I told her, 'and it's just a year long with full government funding.' She was perhaps even poorer than me and I once gave her some of my old clothes as hers were tattered and she didn't have enough spare cash to buy more even in the charity shops. Unlike me, however, she did actually manage to get an audition and went off on an odyssey of a train journey that she could scarcely afford. I'd urged her to ask them to cover her ticket when she arrived but she'd been too shy to do so. It was fortunate that she didn't listen to my sensible advice to become a teacher and persevered as she got the part and ultimately became a highly successful stage actor. Meanwhile, being in our lacklustre production, had made me more interested in directing and I hoped that by becoming a drama teacher, I'd be able to direct whatever plays I liked how I liked, all the while earning a steady wage in a secure career.

17

Scones & the Consummation of Intimacy

Soon after *The Mystery Plays* run had ended, I walked past a funny little cafe called World of Scones, so named because it claimed to sell every variety of scone on the planet. There I heard a familiar voice, 'Would you like a sultana scone, a cheese scone, a cranberry scone, an oatmeal scone, a raisin scone, a cherry scone, a chocolate scone... erm...an orange or lemon peel, I mean zest scone, a cinnamon scone or just a plain old plain scone?'

I nipped down the snicket to the outdoor seating in the courtyard to see Jay in his mallard tie, but now in a waiter's apron instead of a tweed jacket. He saw me and ducked inside. I waited by the honey-suckle until he came out again with a tray of scones. After he'd served the table, he sheepishly came over to me.

'What the heck are you doing here reeling off lists of scones?' I asked.

'Well, they make us memorise them; there are no menus, you see,' he semi-explained.

'But what about your usual job writing pamphlets about dog harnesses?'

'Ah, that. Well, I was no good at bringing in new

clients, you see. Chatterboxes often are but I just liked to talk with potential customers. I never pressured them to sign on the dotted line so they didn't and I got made redundant. I can't get the dole so I had to get another job right away. This was the only one I could find. I didn't want you to know. I thought you'd think I was a nitwit.'

'Why would that bother me when I'm a lowly wait-ress myself? And are there any perks with the job like free scones?'

'Indeed there are,' he winked, 'I'll drop by with some tonight on my way home.'

'And I'll provide the jam!' I proclaimed.

It wasn't such a problem that Jay only brought the plain variety. On this new equal footing in the cater-ing industry, and to my great surprise after many purely platonic months, our love of scones suddenly united us in a new sense. My touch-paper was finally ignited, crackling into life and flaring up to the heavens to Händel's *Royal Fireworks Overture*, at least in my imagination. My reaction at the formerly elusive key moment, was to burst out laughing because this new sensation was certainly not like any fairground ride I'd been on.

I later wondered what, other than scones, brought this sexual revolution about for me. Was it that, for the first time, I'd allowed myself to venture into being passionate with someone with whom I'd become a close friend beforehand? Or was it more that Jay, unlike the others, could think beyond his own gratification? I recalled a short passage entitled 'How to Conduct Oneself in Intimacy', in *A Young Lady's Miscellany* by yet another anonymous writer only giving his identity as 'A Clergyman from the South Downs'. Reading this as a young teenager with little understanding of the subtext, I remembered a generally positive tone in support of husband and wife being 'as one' and 'finding pleasure in each other'. There was a note of caution, however, in the vein of too much of a good thing is not good for the purity of the soul, and urging separate bedrooms for half the week at the very least. Unfortunately, this wasn't the case as, from this time, Jay spent every night at my bedsit.

I wondered whether Manda and May in their younger days had ever peaked in passion. Of course, Manda, with her voracious appetite for Mills and Boon paperbacks, particularly those with quite tempestuous cover art, clearly had a passionate soul which I hope found satisfaction. As for May, the only reading material I saw her with was one of the more sedate tabloids which gave no clues to any hidden desires.

Jay was curious to see more of the north of England so we went off on day trips whenever we had a little money and time to spare and had some unusual episodes, frequently of an amorous nature. En route to the Lincolnshire Wolds, we shared an improbable erotic moment in a train toilet outside Goole. On another occasion, we found a conveniently located study booth in a deserted historical library but didn't get round to reading. One time, having in mind some al fresco titillation, he led me off the primrose path of virtue in Hardcastle Crags, after which I stepped on a nest of miner bees in the undergrowth and had to leap into a nearby river to escape their apian wrath.

There was one incident during this honeymoon period about which I have mixed feelings. I look back upon it with a paradoxical mixture of remorse and pride, reflecting upon my ability to conduct myself so shamelessly. Jay and I had gone to see a production of *Macbeth* in Hull which ended later than anticipated so that we missed the last train back to York. The streets were freezing and dotted with dangerous looking assemblages of young men so we had to think fast. With it being late and with us not having the money between us to stay in one of the few city centre hotels, I had an idea. I recalled that Dreary from college hailed from Hull and so resolved that I'd test her Christian charity by giving her a ring and explaining that we were stranded on her home turf. I obtained her number from Directory Enquiries and called her house but her elderly father said she wasn't home. This, I deduced on the spot, was actually going to work to our advantage. 'Oh, gosh, really? It's just that she said if I was ever in Hull, I absolutely must come and stay!' Naturally, she never would have said this to me. Jay, himself a practiced master of shameless behaviour when the need arose, was quite flabbergasted by my audacity.

We took a bus over to a 'dreary' little estate and were welcomed by her parents who rustled up some Heinz tomato soup accompanied by toast with margarine on their best china. They told us that Dreary usually got back from her Bible study group after eleven which I thought seemed odd, as if she might be up to something else under the cover of her religious meditation, but I chose not to voice my suspicions. While we ate, I regaled the parents with fictional stories of all the fun Dreary and I had had in our college days. The highlight of the night came when she returned from her 'Bible study group' at the late hour of midnight. Her jaw gaped and her eyes popped yet, quite admirably, she responded to our plight sympathetically and maintained the composure to receive us with good grace.

Being under a Christian roof, Jay slept in the tiny box room, while I slept in the other bed in Dreary's twin room and acted as if we had been on friendly terms in college which I could see mystified her. I told Dreary I had recently been in a Biblical play in an attempt to pique her sense of camaraderie. She asked me what part I had played, to which I responded, 'Why Eve, the temptress, cause of mankind's fall.' She smiled and nodded, remaining politely confused until we left her house after breakfast the following morning. I wondered if, at that moment, she would have let on to her parents that she'd always found me disagreeable. Jay tipped his hat to me, whom he now saw as more than a match for him in roguery.

Although there was at last more to sex than procreation, having been careless about contraception on a couple of occasions, only a month later, I found myself expecting. Fortunately, the bundle of joy would be arriving when my teaching course at Huddersfield University was coming to an end.

We left our respective digs and went to live with Dave, Jay's closest friend in York, until we had saved enough money to put down a deposit on a rented place of our own. I started commuting to

Huddersfield where I would be working towards a teaching qualification. This commute wasn't easy because the frequent lurching of the train triggered my morning sickness.

Living with Dave at this juncture also wasn't easy as there were further triggers connected to him. He kept a bowl of goldfish and the sight of the long threads of their excrement hanging from their bodies and flowing along behind them, made me retch on the spot. The other problem was that a medication Dave took made him severely constipated, from which uncomfortable con-dition he found some relief by jesting about it, which used to make me feel queasy. One day, having met with defecatory success after a dry spell lasting some days, he helped us to visualize his tormented excreta by describing it as 'seagulls' heads' in both size and shape.

I was also regularly stricken just by looking at certain photographs. Curious as to how things were going along within my womb, I would go into a particular bookshop and leaf through books with giant colour images of the foetus at different stages of development where I would be horrified by the little jelly bean creatures with their raisin eyes. The reason I patronised this specific bookshop was that it had a toilet into which I could rush when overcome.

I decided to call Manda with the news. When she'd turned eighty, she'd had a phone installed in her house at her son, Eric's insistence. Before that, when she or Wiff had needed to use a phone, which was seldom, they'd go to the phone box on the corner. Manda wasn't very good on the phone and never learnt telephone etiquette. She still spoke hastily when on a call, as she used to on the pay phone, putting the receiver down abruptly without saying goodbye in the hope the unused coins would drop out. For this reason, I'd have preferred to have written or visited her in person with my news but, unable to afford the train fare, I called as I wanted to hear her voice. I was excited to tell her about the pregnancy but was hurt when she was brusque with me, which I'd never previously known her to be, responding with, 'It'd be better if you were married!' It was not like her and I wondered whether someone, my father for example, had said this to her and she was just parroting it.

Of course, I was merely continuing an unspoken tradition of unmarried mothers in the family. I must have been about twelve when, rummaging through a shoe box of photos in the bureau in Caerleon, I chanced upon my parents' wedding photograph. I was puzzled that my mother was in a smart grey suit instead of the archetypal white dress, and that there were only a handful of guests. Turning the photograph over, I found the date written in May's sloping handwriting, and even with my rudimentary grasp of mathematics, I deduced that my mother was already a few months pregnant with my eldest sister. I suddenly saw my parents' relationship in a new light, as that of two people who'd been forced to get married as teenagers who had never been particularly well suited to one another or happy together. I didn't reveal my discovery to my mother for some time and when I finally did, she told me that May's first reaction on hearing the news of her out-of-wedlock pregnancy was to give her a whack with the wicker carpet beater. Years later, when my mother finally plucked up the courage to ask her why she'd done that, May told her, 'I was upset because I always wanted to make you a wedding dress, and for you to get married in white and in a church just like I had.'

Whenever my mother's family had taken a trip to Rochdale, May's home town, she would point out the church where she'd married Joseph, and would describe her glorious dress, the flowers and the wedding breakfast afterwards. Accordingly, after her mother died, my mother went over to Rochdale in her honour. She hadn't been back there for over twenty years. She went to see the house where May was born, a cottage within a brewery owned by her grandfather, and then walked over to the graves of May's parents. In the afternoon, she went to the church and, having never actually been inside, walked down the aisle imagining her mother in her flowing white dress, like her namesake, Princess May of Teck. My mother then got to chatting with the verger, who invited her to look up the marriage entry in the parish register. Unfortunately, she couldn't find it on the date she'd known all her life to be her parents' wedding anniversary. 'Could there be a mistake?' the verger had asked. To be sure, they looked over the weeks before and after, but found not a trace of the wedding. Finally, the verger suggested she go to the town hall and check the registry office records but my mother knew for a fact her parents had married in that very church. It had always been pointed out when they visited Rochdale, she told him. The verger had shrugged and urged her to check anyway. She duly did so, starting with the date of the anniversary, but then skimming over earlier and later dates until she finally discovered Joseph and May, only there would have been three in the family by then because May was already pregnant with Jim.

In spite of the years of moral coaching from *A Young Lady's Miscellany*, May had let down her guard for a moment. Joseph, a handsome military man, probably traumatised to some extent, had taken an interest in her, a bespectacled shop girl. She must have temporarily relaxed her Victorian propriety and seized the day. The shame of pre-marital relations and the shotgun wedding would have been too much to bear so she had invented the fairytale of the church and the white dress. Over time, perhaps, her story had become more and more vivid in her imagination until barely a grain of truth remained. She must have been jolted to the core when her only daughter re-enacted it.

So there I was—the third generation of out-of-wedlock pregnancies. Heaven knows what May would have made of my boyfriend, long-haired and American. Knowing 'the trouble' he'd got her youngest granddaughter into, she'd probably have condemned him to be 'put up against a brick wall and shot', just as she had once wished upon those reprobates, The New Seekers, with their long, loose hair.

18

A Suitable Career for the Fallen Woman

We rented a terraced house, smaller than Manda's, in the village of Marsden in the Pennine Mountains of West Yorkshire, a short train ride to Huddersfield. The weather was always rainy and we even had newts and toads in the little damp cellar where the washing machine sat. Other than kitchen appliances and a dining table and chairs, the house was entirely empty of furniture. We slept on a couple of quilts on the bedroom carpet, and got by on my government grant and Jay's new freelance work for a man in Manchester who was in the business of starting up local radio stations.

Up the hill from us was the famous Butterley Reservoir with its ornamental stepped cascade that flowed down to power Marsden's sole remaining working mill at the bottom of the slope. There was a plaque on the wall of the reservoir commemorating the ceremonial 'cutting of the first sod' by an Alderman of the time, almost one hundred years before we arrived there. A hundred years before work started on the reservoir, Marsden had witnessed the excavation of the longest canal tunnel in England. The process of using picks, shovels and gunpowder to cut through the mountain had left many dead, overshot two bank deadlines and required two government bailouts. Like all early canal tunnels, this one was so narrow and low that there was no room for the draft horses to come through. Instead, the narrowboat workers would take their horses over the mountain, while the boat was navigated through the tunnel by professional 'leggers', who lay on their backs against the opposing gunnels of the boat with their feet against the tunnel wall, 'legging it' along. This mainly occurred in total darkness and took up to three hours, depending on how heavy the load was.

When we came to live in Marsden, nearly two hundred years after the excavation was complete, the mouth of the tunnel had been boarded up for over fifty years. In the year we lived there, we witnessed the early stages of another burst of prosperity, this time in property development, whereby the derelict mills were being turned into stylish apartments with 'a wealth of original features' as Marsden became popular with commuters working in the nearby cities.

In Marsden, we became friends with David and Julie, an unusual couple who lived with their two-year-old, Lulu, in a house renovated and decorated so as to be in a 1950s time-warp. Their sitting room had plaster casts adorning the walls depicting full-figured women with cat-eye make-up, holding candelabras. Their kitchen was kitted out with vintage cabinets they'd found in second-hand shops. Apart from May's, it was the only non-fitted kitchen I'd seen. Julie wore clothes from her favourite epoch, full pleated skirts, brightly coloured floral dresses and large yellow plastic earrings. Lulu, who was often addressed by her parents as 'Chicken Dinner', was likewise dressed in 1950s children's wear.

Huddersfield University had tried to persuade me to enrol on their primary teaching qualification course as there was something of a national shortage at the time. I resisted their entreaties, not only because I wanted to direct school plays, but also due to not wanting to follow in the footsteps of the teacher I'd had for my first two years of school, the cruel Miss Read. Although her name sounded like that of a teacher from the Happy Families children's card game, she was never happy. She wore her hair scraped back into a large grey bun like a wasps' nest and those little stinging creatures metaphorically whizzed about her in the swarms of unkind words she had for the little children in her class. We did a lot of cross-stitch with Miss Read, which was appropriate because she was very cross indeed if someone made a mistake. 'What a stu-pid child!' she would chide, standing over them and unpicking their work. She sought ways to humiliate children, particularly a little boy called Stewart who often came to school with his shoes on the wrong feet. She would whisk him up onto a desk and encourage us to laugh at him.

Miss Read's classroom was in a little building apart from the rest of the school, like a witch's cottage but without decorations made of sweets. At lunchtime she would lock it with a big, old fashioned key but one rainy day she accidentally left the door unlocked. The class crept inside to shelter from the

foul weather and at first, everyone was well behav-
ed, as if Miss Read were present. Soon, however, we
became anarchic, jumping from desk to desk, relishing our freedom from her tyranny. I didn't want Miss
Read to come back, not merely because I was afraid
of what she'd do to us when she did, but also because
this was a rare moment when school was actually
fun. So, without anyone noticing, I went up on my
tiptoes and bolted the door, to prolong the mayhem,
as much as to put off the reign of terror that was
sure to follow.

Eventually, out of the corner of my eye, I spotted
Miss Read coming into view, a hunched witch's shadow in the frosted glass of the door. At first, she only
loomed there, rattling the handle. Soon though, she
began bashing the door, howling to be let in. When
my classmates finally heard her, they gingerly got
down from the desks and began gathering around
the door, confused because it wouldn't open. Their
expressions turned desperate and nobody thought to
check the bolt above. It became painful to watch the
intensifying terror and, finally, I could not let it
continue any longer. With a smidgen of early acting
promise, I put surprise in my voice and exclaimed,
'Look, someone's bolted the door!' I stretched up to
open it and Miss Read barged in, pushing me aside.

Through gritted teeth in a furious, hissing voice
she demanded repeatedly, 'Who bolted the door?
Who bolted the door?'

Certain that it would be a caning offence, I held
my tongue and shrugged, perhaps a little too hard,
whispering to children near me, 'Did you do it?', at
which they hurriedly shook their terrified little

heads. It was in this instant that I realised that even though lying is bad, sometimes it is essential.

After a few months of classes at the university, I began my teaching practice at a sixth form college in Wakefield. On the day I was due to start, the train halted a few miles outside Wakefield after it seemed to trip over an obstruction on the track. We passengers waited quietly for it to start again, while I became concerned about turning up late on my first day. Twenty minutes later, emergency services arrived and I feared, with the appearance of paramedics, that the obstruction we'd gone over had been a person. I waited for the strangely dressed men with the coffin to appear like the previous time I'd come across a death on the tracks half my life ago, but the approach here lacked any archaic ceremony with just a plain black plastic body bag and only people in yellow high vis jackets milling around.

The carriage I was in was largely empty but there was a young man in an ill-fitting suit sitting across the aisle from me starting to hyperventilate. A small train engine drew up alongside and a policeman boarded our carriage then told us what had happened. He went on to say that there was no possibility of the train moving for some time but added, 'We will now take anyone off the train who is pregnant.' The hyperventilating man behind me beat me to the buzzer, shooting up his hand and shouting 'Me!' Fortunately, even though there wasn't yet much evidence of my pregnancy, they took me, and only me, onward to the next station by way of the little engine. The sensation of the train going over the person lingered for some years.

Julie, as fascinated by death as by the 1950s, listened eagerly to my retelling of these events. She had aspirations to work for a funeral director one day. Whenever she saw fresh flowers on a newly dug grave, she was compelled to find out who had died.

Due to my pregnant cravings for spicy food, Jay and I would sometimes make the lengthy journey to Bobby's, a celebrated little Indian cafe in Leeds. It was in a run-down area on the outskirts of the city and, once the bus dropped us off, there was a long walk, much of it over waste ground. The only Indian food I'd had before this had been as an eight-year-old at a local restaurant in Selby where we'd gone on a rare family outing in honour of my older sister receiving a university offer. The elderly waiter, excessively fawning, probably because we were the only customers, had given us each a gristly rissole of a greenish hue, constructed from unfamiliar meat and spices and served atop a leaf of iceberg lettuce. This had put me off Indian food for many years. Bobby's, however, cured me of this early aversion as it was wonderful in flavour, price and generosity of portions and always rounded off with glorious Indian desserts and lassis.

We had some money to spare over the Christmas holidays so Jay and I ambled into a travel agent in Huddersfield to peruse their last minute deals. We wanted to get away from the British Christmas hype, along with going somewhere warmer as winter weather in Marsden was generally characterised by sleety stair rods and slushy snows. Julie and David couldn't understand our aversion to the Brontesque Pennine weather as they loved rain, mist and cold and went on more ambitious walks than us in it, the whole family decked out in 1950s woolens, with Lulu often embellishing her dowdy duffle coat with a tutu.

We settled on a two-week package holiday to Malta, the cheapest on offer. It would be my first time on a plane and, as it turned out, a propeller plane at that. The force of take off came as a surprise, especially as I hadn't read any books warning me about what it was going to be like. Being in a propeller aircraft, our flight took around five hours and, on our arrival in Malta, the warm winter sun was lovely. What we had never anticipated was that Christmas hype there was worse than in England.

On every street, music piped through crackling tannoys declared a wish for it to be 'Christmas every day'. Then there was Slade's misleading boast, 'So here it is, Merry Christmas, everybody's having fun', at which I kept thinking, 'Well, I might be, if you would stop.' Shop windows had unsettling flashing decorations and residential houses a plethora of plastic models of reindeer and inflatable snowmen.

We managed to escape by getting on one of the old minibuses, all polished chrome and festooned with images of the saints, that went out to the Neolithic temples situated in the deserted parts of the island. I was pleased to learn that primitive Malta was thought to have been a matriarchal society that worshipped a full-bodied she-deity whose fecund shape my own form had begun to emulate. We had these ancient sites to ourselves as it was off-season.

Back in Valletta, where our accommodation was

situated, we did our best to avoid the festivities, sitting in cafes in back alleys where they made the hot chocolate thick, dark and barely sweetened. We also partook of the carbonated drink, Kinnie, made from the island's bitter oranges and wormwood. The honey from Malta, produced by bee-keepers on a small scale, was miraculous. When Dave visited us on our return, he finished a whole jar in one sitting.

Returning to my teaching practice in Wakefield after the holiday, a student in my drama class called out that old favourite, 'Let's put on a play!', to which I responded with a foolhardy, 'Yes, let's!' without fully realising the immense undertaking it would be in my soon-to-be heavily laden state. I was already wearing a swimming costume under my clothes because I didn't like the way my stomach oscillated when I walked. I had also become less energetic, unable to stay awake after 9 pm. Still, in a bid to be cutting edge, I scoured the library for a lesser-known play for my enthusiastic drama group and discovered a pair of one acts by the French Absurdist, Eugene Ionesco, *The Future is in Eggs* and *Jacques or Obedience*. They were ensemble pieces that parodied provincial middle class family life, and were, therefore, perfect for my eighteen-year-old drama students who were in the throes of cynicism about the adult world.

Out of the blue, a regular interruption to my common-law married bliss began arriving in the form of a weekly letter appearing on our doormat from the girlfriend who'd shoved Jay out of her car in York two and a half years earlier and who was now regretting her actions. He had sent a reply informing her that he was now embarking upon a family life with a calmer, kinder woman but that didn't deter her. In her letters, she would fondly reminisce on the good old days, even though these had, according to Jay, become increasingly fraught as time had gone on. She liked to enclose autumn leaves in the envelopes, pertaining to some nostalgia they shared. He brushed it aside as something not to worry about but, all the same, the idea of raising a child alone alarmed me. The ex-girlfriend had even phoned once and summed me up as someone who had 'too many vowels' in their name. Although Jay had told her to stop, she didn't. Ultimately, my insecurities prompted me to rush off a postcard to her from the point of view of the foetus accompanied by an accurate sketch of one in the second trimester. Her letters then ceased.

The Ionesco double-bill featured physical theatre in the form of humorous coordinated automata-like movement. I'd enjoyed my first proper ensemble directing experience and it was suggested to me by the Head of Drama at the college that we might want to put it on again at the Edinburgh Fringe that summer. Heavily pregnant though I was, I shared his enthusiasm and we started to plan the trip. By the time I fully took into account that I'd be the only person available to operate the sound and lighting with a newborn in tow, it was too late.

Whenever I had time, I went into bookshops and leafed through the pages of the books about giving birth, which were often illustrated with glossy pictures. I couldn't afford to buy such books to pore over further at home but it didn't matter because, as

I soon realised, they would barely give me a taste of the reality of the experience. I had decided for sure, that I didn't want the epidural injection in my spine, not only because that in itself conjured up a nasty image, but also because the thinking at the time was that it led to a higher likelihood of cerebral palsy and, recalling how Jo suffered, I preferred to go through hours of pain rather than inflict on anyone what she'd had to endure for a lifetime.

There was an indoor market in Huddersfield where we used to buy poppyseed cake from a Polish food stall. I'd eaten some for supper the night before and the following morning there came the first hint of the oncoming storm as my stomach decided to purge itself of its contents which consisted solely of poppyseeds. Within two hours, we were at the hospital, where we waited fifteen hours for the slow dilation. I became more and more nervous as the time passed which resulted in the baby's heartbeat going off the scale in reaction to my stress.

Eventually, the obstetrician was called over and something I hadn't read about happened. A heart monitoring wire was put up me and slipped under the skin of the baby's head. This meant I had to remain motionless on a gurney, belted into place, which only made matters worse. The cylinder of gas and air provided some relief against the intensifying pain which was comparable to a form of medieval torture in which the legs are gradually dislocated from the pelvis. In camaraderie, Jay had a few puffs on the gas and air too and promptly became no use to anyone, giggling to himself in the corner. The terrible spasms finally became too much and I was rolled off toward the agreeably named 'delivery suite', clearly so-called to disguise that it was a place of excruciating pain. As I was being wheeled, I still had the nozzle for the gas and air cylinder in my mouth and was inhaling on it deeply without realising it had been disconnected from the cylinder. When Jay tried to alert the nurse to this, she shushed him as if I weren't present, plainly hoping I'd keep using it as a placebo.

I was unlucky with the midwife who was assigned to me that night. There was a line of 'delivery suites', each with the door shut but, by the sound of it, containing a woman in the agonising throes of labour which, to my extreme trepidation, was shortly to be me. My allotted midwife strolled in, all smiles and lipstick, her thick, dyed black hair in a large up-do under her white hat, and wearing a cinched nurse's uniform to enhance her curves. I could see she was one of those no-nonsense types who'd long since lost all sense of empathy for her suffering charges. She immediately brought out the epidural needle and advanced toward me.

'No, no!' I cried, the needle just inches from my spine.

'What? Everyone has them but, if you insist, then suit yourself,' she scoffed. She then took a look up my surgical gown. 'You're not very far on, are you? I don't know why they've even brought you in as we've scarcely enough delivery suites as it is.'

With that, she turned on her heel and left the room, leaving me feeling guilt-ridden for being there. Half an hour passed and things were getting more and more uncomfortable. The midwife returned, breezing in with a dismissive, 'I could hear you right down the corridor! Don't you think you're being a bit of a drama queen? I could still give you that epidural, you know.'

Being a newly qualified drama teacher, I considered 'drama queen' to be more of an accolade than an insult but, as it happened, the insult was now irrelevant. Having been in hospital for over fourteen hours, the time had finally come for the first push. I had heard other women compare having a baby to passing a grapefruit, with some even likening it to a watermelon, but this infant was more akin to a pineapple. As the head began to emerge, small lacerations pinged as they proliferated like a child's too small mitten unravelling.

Once the head was out, the midwife said, 'What a nice little boy!' I was confused, therefore, when the whole baby emerged and a girl was presented to me. She had a strange odour of cardboard that had been left out in the rain, but was otherwise quite perfect. She didn't look like the terribly wrinkled newborns I'd seen in the books, all splattered with blood, coated in waxy-looking stuff and with the mis-shapen head so many of them have, bent into a sort of stuffed letter C by the sheer force of the vagina. She was as glossy as a pearl, with wide-open eyes in a firm little face and there was no crying whatsoever, unlike newborns in the movies. The umbilical cord, much longer than I'd anticipated, was an uneven grey, the colour of Wrigley's Spearmint Gum, and twisted into a corkscrew, exactly the way I used to put the gum sticks into my mouth as a child.

The time of birth was recorded as 00.01 and, very

soon afterwards, the midwife had ushered the confused Jay out, telling him to 'get off with ye lad. Go
on home now'. She ordered me to be wheeled into a
ward where the baby was placed next to me in a
clear plastic crib on wheels. I was handed a mug of
milky tea as a means of recovery and told to go to
sleep. Instead, for the next few hours, I stared at the
baby, repeatedly checking that she was still breathing. She didn't sleep either, being transfixed by the
little orange light on the nurse's buzzer by my bed.
At regular intervals, she'd raise and tremble her tiny
arms, no doubt some habit left over from having to
keep moving in the womb. At around three, I needed
to relieve myself after the milky tea so I hobbled
over to the bathrooms off the ward. Here was something else they'd missed out of the books...urination
and laceration are incompatible and their combination will result in agony upon the lavatory.

Come the morning, I had the task of changing the
baby, which was a completely new experience for me.
Greenish meconium had flowed out of her nappy up
to her neck and she was screaming as I attempted to
put her to rights with a packet of wipes. The midwife
who'd delivered her suddenly appeared in the
commotion but kept her distance, preferring to
regard the scene from afar, whilst leaning on the
door frame. She made no effort to offer advice,
coming out with the laconic observation, 'You've got
your work cut out, haven't you?' It was all a bit much
to bear, with my walking problems after the attack
of the nibbling pineapple, and I was determined to
leave as soon as possible so that Jay could help me
at home. When he arrived in the afternoon, he was,

like me, a touch befuddled by lack of sleep. He'd brought me some clothes, but the bag he carried contained mainly bras. I had no idea I owned so many bras. It was as if he now unconsciously saw me as some multi-teated fertility deity.

I left the hospital the next day and my mother visited our largely furniture-free house, bearing a baby's cot and a box of special sea salt crystals to put in my bath so I could soothe my ragged undercarriage. I didn't yet have a name for the baby as I was daunted by the responsibility of it so I was calling her Geoffrey in the meantime. Seated in our impractical half-sized bathtub, I looked over the lists of wildly extravagant names we'd jotted down over the past few months: Hepzibah, Kezia, Axolotl, Cosmo, all of which now seemed far too overwhelming, and possibly cruel, to give to a tiny baby. I wished she'd come out with a name stamped on her behind so that would have been that.

Despite her being unnamed, and despite being unused to babies, holding her soon gave me a sense of peace I couldn't remember knowing before. Gone were any lingering thoughts of one day scraping a living through professional acting, which would probably mean often working away from home and worrying about her.

Two months later we were heading to Edinburgh by train with six teenagers for a four day trip to the Fringe Festival. Jay had taken on the grotesque bit-part of Grandfather as the student playing that hadn't been able to come. Jay would be on stage the whole time, sitting behind a gilt frame as a sort of living portrait, occasionally coming out with some snippet of absurd dialogue. I'd be doing the lights and sound at the back but thanks to the baby's tranquil nature, this proved easier than I'd expected.

The students did the usual thing for Edinburgh Fringe actors and trawled through the crowds in the streets handing out flyers to promote the show because we hadn't sold many tickets. This seemed to be the norm at the Fringe where the actors often outnumbered the audience. The students also decided to perform some extracts in costume in the street in an effort to gather interest.

Also performing at our venue was a one woman show based on the writings of Virginia Woolf, with an actress pretending to be her. Bits out of Woolf's essays and letters were to be read aloud in the author's costume and accent. I wasn't sure how this could be classed as a show and felt badly that the actress would probably have an even smaller audience than us. She thought so too and kindly offered our student troupe complimentary tickets. However, on arrival, we were astonished to find there was standing room only. The room was full of feminist Virginia Woolf devotees who gave off an excited vibe, as if the spirit of the celebrated author was soon to be raised in their midst. The lights went up and the woman strolled in wearing a typically Woolfian gigantic hat with a 1920s style dress and delivered the sacred words. She hadn't even memorized the extracts. She just read them from a paper on her lectern. Thirty minutes later, it was all over and there was uproarious applause. I was left musing upon the months of work these teenagers and I had put into our superb ensemble piece, only for it to be largely overlooked in favour of an offering like this that required no real effort other than getting a posh Bloomsbury drawl right and sourcing a very large hat. The tragic truth was Virginia Woolf, with her faithful following among the British chattering classes, was bound to triumph over two lesser-known plays by the lesser-known, Eugene Ionesco. Audiences, even ostensibly 'artsy' ones like those at the Fringe, will invariably favour the famous or familiar and our plays and players were the antithesis of that.

A similar example of a weak show drawing a full house due to being familiar was the curiously named *One Man Hamlet*. Jay and I went along, not entirely understanding what it could be. Imagine our disappointment when it turned out to be an untalented actor doing Hamlet's soliloquies knitted together with linking bits of the play in an hour of droning self-importance. Nevertheless, a great comic moment came after the show when an American tourist, in all seriousness, approached the actor and asked, 'Is this your own material?'. Poor Jay cringed in shame at the infamous ignorance of his compatriots, which he said beat hands down that of the British who generally had at least some notion of the literary landmarks of their own language, if no one else's.

After Edinburgh, Jay and I took separate trains. He would go back to Marsden where he'd had some freelance editing sent to him and I decided to do a dog leg and stop off at Whitehaven for a few days so Manda could meet the baby. I was a little apprehensive after Manda's 'It'd be better if you were married' comment and hoped she hadn't turned into

a different sort of person. I went through her unlocked front door, across the parlour and there she
was, sitting in front of the gas fire with tea in a
china beaker and reading one of her Mills and Boon
books. This one, *Marry In Haste*, seemed fitting in
light of our last conversation on the telephone. It
turned out that I had nothing to worry about. She
was so happy to see me and loved all babies, even the
out-of-wedlock variety.

While Manda prepared some toast with rum
butter at my nostalgic request, I went out of the back
door intending to take a quick stroll in the meadow. I
was shocked to see newly-laid concrete foundations,
one of them smothering our beloved blackcurrant
bushes. Leaning through the kitchen window, I
asked Manda what on earth was going on and she
told me that some houses were being built and would
be finished within the next twelve months. Scanning
the landscape further, things only became worse.
Sen had died recently and I saw across the meadow
that his pigeon loft had been razed to the ground. A
high, chainlink fence topped with razor wire now
lined the perimeter of what had become a carport
belonging to his long-estranged son who had inherited the place.

Manda's introverted neighbour, Mr Priestly, who
had more than a passing likeness to Alfred Hitchock,
peered over the whitewashed yard wall, with just his
eyes and bald pate visible. Previously, he'd been
someone who would shyly say hello at the most
before beetling indoors, but now he seemed eager to
chat. His gregarious sister, with whom he'd always
shared a house, had died and, because she'd always

done all the talking for him, he barely spoke. Just before I went inside, he asked me to wait for a present he had for the baby. He nervously passed this over the wall. It was a nice little painted wood wall-hanging that someone from his work had once brought back for him from Croatia, featuring a goose girl and her geese. He'd kept it in a drawer not knowing what to do with it.

When I returned inside, I showed it to Manda who remarked, 'Oh, that's nice, where shall I put it?' Not thinking it through, I told her the truth that it was from Mr Priestly for the baby. When Manda died, it was one of my regrets that I hadn't given it to her there and then. On the day after her funeral, I would put it on her grave.

19

Tribulations among the In-Laws of North America

The time had come to meet the in-laws, despite not being married. Jay's mother, Jane, had received the news of his new girlfriend's pregnancy with horror, 'Make me that baby's guardian!' she had yelled down the phone when Jay first informed her of the milestone, which revealed her complete lack of confidence in her son's capability to be a decent father. He was her only child and had been given a first class private education, which had led to a promising job on Wall Street once she'd pulled a few strings. What a lack of gratitude and common sense he had shown, therefore, when, only two months after starting his stock market training programme, he'd decamped to embark upon a round the world trip, with a view, kept from her, to probably never return. Seven years after his graduation from one of the 'elite' American liberal arts colleges, she was puzzled as to why he hadn't yet shaken off this wanderlust and continued to move from job to job, none of them with prospects. Despite never asking her for any kind of support, she had still decided that he was unfit to be either a father or a connubial partner. I, on the other hand, saw the opposite of

240

this—a man who was determined to take on an equal share in caring for a child both financially and emotionally, even if we only just made ends meet and owned next to nothing.

When Jane had given birth to Jay, it had been a near-death experience for her that she never wished to repeat. His conception had been a thinly-veiled plot to save her failing marriage, which had taken place when she and Jay's father were turning twenty-one in the 1950s. Since that time, her young husband's outlook on life had been profoundly altered by the societal changes of the 1960s, whilst hers had not.

Jane had named her son so he would have the same initials as her in order that he could, one day, inherit her monogrammed tableware. It irked her that he wanted to live in distant countries and preferred a lifestyle devoid of formal dinner parties because this made her long-term planning in such matters redundant. Jay maintained that in giving him her initials there was also an element of expecting him to be a male version of herself and when he'd ultimately turned out to be very different, it had been difficult for her to endure.

She tended to place the blame squarely on the shoulders of his father, who had walked out on her when Jay was a toddler, and transitioned from man in a grey flannel suit to one in blue denim, in a decade-long foray into hippy culture that, in Jane's mind, had fatally tainted Jay's emergent personality. Some of Jay's most vivid childhood memories were of weekends or vacations away visiting his father, when he would sometimes be taken on voyages in a

converted truck into the countryside to attend
'happenings' or 'gatherings', where he would mix, oh
the horror, with children who went to state school, or
worse, did not go to school at all.

Since the final trimester of my pregnancy, Jane
had been offering to buy us air tickets to New York
so that she could meet the new grandchild she was
still convinced she'd have to adopt sooner or later.
The plan was that we'd stay with 'Grandma Jane' in
the apartment where Jay had grown up, for the two
week duration of the visit. I had reluctantly agreed
but it was a very long flight for a four-month-old
baby. So, in August, a couple of weeks after our
Edinburgh trip, we set out on the odyssey.

The journey ended up being all the more taxing
because we had to share a bank of seats with an
unusual family. The dad was a mannequin-perfect
American in a roll-neck who'd been on sabbatical for
six months studying British lichen. The mum was
dowdy in comparison in stretched clothes and wonky
glasses. Their toddler, Penina, possibly named after
the two parts of the body that had brought about her
existence, had her parents wrapped around her
chubby little finger. When presented with the lunch
menu, they simperingly asked her if she'd like the
chicken or the pasta dish and, overwhelmed by the
choice, she rolled on the floor screaming. As she did
this, she yanked her mother's clothing which was
probably why it was baggy. Nevertheless, it proved a
useful insight into children and the notion of choice.

When we landed in New York, Jane was standing
behind the barrier in arrivals. My first impression
was of a diminutive, tense lady, with a straw roof of

coarse hair. 'The car is that way! Walk over there!' she'd yapped, sticking out an arm to the right, without even saying hello. When we met her again at the car, she didn't even glance at the grandchild she'd insisted she was so desperate to see, instead looking Jay up and down in disdain. He'd been trying to live up to her expectations to some extent by looking smart on his return to his hometown, and had bought a linen suit from one of Huddersfield's many charity shops. It was from a quality suit maker and had been very expensive in its day but, unfortunately, had become crumpled en route, as linen is wont to do.

'Unshaven, as usual, I see. And what are you wearing?' she scoffed, 'You look like Ratso Rizzo in *Midnight Cowboy!*'

As we sped off toward Manhattan, I saw Jay stifling tears of humiliation and wondered what on earth I had common-law married into.

We stopped in front of one of the hundreds of apartment blocks we'd been gliding past, where a uniformed doorman rushed up to open the car door for us. We then walked through a lavish lobby with a marble floor, smoked mirror walls, a fountain and ornamental ferns.

Up in the apartment, the first thing I saw when I stepped inside were two framed Javanese shadow puppets made of leather that Jay had mentioned having sent his mother during his travels, which had been delayed in the international postal system for so many months that he had returned home to visit before they'd arrived. The main room featured a glass, steel and oak Bauhaus dining table, a walnut veneered antique desk, modern Scandinavian-style bookshelves in rosewood, a vintage Eames lounge chair with footstool, a contemporary glass Tiffany lamp in the shape of a mushroom on an occasional table, and a pair of capacious couches upholstered in a soft looking cream-coloured fabric. Jay had told me that nothing had changed in this room for a quarter of a century when Jane had redecorated it so as to remove all reminders of her first marriage.

Exhausted after a journey that had lasted nearly twenty-four hours door to door, I made a beeline for the larger of the white couches and plonked myself down sitting the baby next to me. From across the room, Jane regarded me with astonishment. Jay, stood behind her, looking anxious, shaking his head and moving his hands up and down, palms up. I didn't understand what he was trying to tell me through mime.

'Jay, didn't you tell her we don't sit on those couches?' Jane reproached him, 'They're upholstered in silk chenille hand woven in Padua! Please, come and sit in my office.'

I upped sticks and followed the two of them into the office, which I already knew, had been Jay's bedroom when he was growing up, but which had been surreptitiously converted to double as her office whilst he was away at that all American institution, summer camp. This was touted to him as his Bar-Mitzvah present but the truth was that Jane was a kindergarten teacher who'd developed a lucrative sideline in 'prepping' small children to get into the nursery schools of their parents' dreams. This was widely considered the first rung on the ladder to a storied place at an Ivy League university fifteen years later, de rigueur among ambitious wealthy people in New York. Jay's bed had turned into a dark green couch and, before he went to school in the morning, he was expected to roll up his bedding and put it away in the walk-in closet, where his clothes and possessions were neatly stowed. If he took anything out, he'd have to put it away before the next morning so that, when Jane returned home from her Kindergarten teaching at 3.30 pm, the room would be 'ready' for her youthful tutees, who were dropped off and picked up by their nannies or, very occasionally, one of their parents. It was in this office, still being used by Jane for her after-school enterprise, that we'd be staying with the baby, so that we were still expected to put away all evidence of our existence each morning in readiness for the arrival of her tiny clients and whichever adult was chaperoning them.

While I was sitting on the green couch, a tall fellow with a pot belly and a bald head entered and introduced himself as Dick. He seated himself in the leather upholstered bucket chair opposite us and Jane automatically handed him a bourbon on the rocks with a bowl of salted pretzel pieces, as if they were a patient's medication administered at a set time in a psychiatric ward. When he finished this, he called out, 'Jane, refresh my drink,' and so she did, quick as a hamster's blurred scratching claw.

Dick held forth about his stellar career in the typography business, as managing director of the company his father had founded in the 1920s. In his youth, he told me, he'd aspired to be a publicist in

245

Hollywood, and had been given a trial period by way of a strategically located relative, but it hadn't worked out. He'd then gone onto Madison Avenue to pursue a career in advertising during its golden age through a business connection of his father's but that hadn't been a success either. The only option left to him had been to work in his father's typographics factory. Half way through his explanation of the sad decline of the once proud typographic industry in the age of computer automation, he sent himself to sleep, thereby rendering the reason for his difficulties in Hollywood and on Madison Avenue fairly clear. He was out cold, but with his eyes still open, looking quite like a wall-eyed grouper, but with a large pale hand, still firmly gripping the glass of half melted ice, balanced on the armrest of the chair.

We sneaked out for a walk and I recalled reading about how the grid pattern of Manhattan's streets had originally been inspired by Whitehaven, back in the days when it was an internationally important port. Whitehaven, in turn, had been inspired by the layout of Ancient Alexandria on the suggestion of Sir Christopher Lowther who had his palatial home in what became Whitehaven's Castle Park. The Ancient World was aware that long, straight roads radiating from busy sea ports were practical whereas the roads intersecting them could be aesthetic with a focal point at the end such as a temple or other striking edifice or even strategically orientated to frame the sunrise or the sunset.

On this walk, I decided to sample my first ever bagel as there was no food in the apartment that we could eat other than sweet or salty snacks in packets. There was a long queue but the service was brisk. The man preparing my bagel couldn't comprehend why I didn't tell him all the fillings I wanted in a rapid fire list at the beginning like all the New Yorkers around me. I confounded him by saying each thing separately, politely giving him time to pick it up, so I thought. 'Hey, lady,' he said, exasperated, arms outstretched, 'Just tell me it togethuh, can't yuh see there's people waitin'?' The hot day had cooled off so we ate our bagels in Central Park, returning to the apartment at 9 pm. Dick and Jane had already gone to bed.

Still on British time, I woke up at 5 am the following morning and looked out of the window, amazed by the morning wave of yellow cabs on the street below, hundreds in the few minutes I watched. I went into the kitchen and made some toast and, when Jay awoke, we immediately put away the bedding. Jane appeared at the bedroom door, looking twitchy. She took Jay to one side and told him in a stage whisper, which I assumed I was intended to hear, to tell me 'not to leave breadcrumbs on the breadboard ever again'.

Jane had planned our day's outing to the Metropolitan Museum followed by lunch in a retro diner-style cafe. Dick stayed home because of his sciatica. In the diner, an elaborately dressed woman with bleached blonde hair and long crimson nails complained that her egg was 'over easy and not sunny-side-up', or it might have been 'sunny-side-up and not over easy'. I didn't understand this new transatlantic egg language. While she spoke in these mysterious nursery rhyme terms, she was raising her voice and standing up, looking most put out. It was mystifying to me that someone could be so perturbed over the preparation of an egg. The waiter, an Hispanic man, took it back as if it were a normal occurrence, no questions asked, or perhaps he thought it was better not to disagree with her.

The next day, Jay, the baby and I did the New York tourist thing and took the ferry to the Statue of Liberty, which was smaller than I'd expected. We then visited the exhibition on Ellis Island where all eight of Jay's great grandparents had been process-ed, escaping various Eastern European persecutions. This was particularly poignant for him and he did his best to hold back the tears. On the way home, we popped into Bloomingdales, the famous department store, where I made the mistake of asking a shop assistant where the toilet was.

'You mean the restroom?' she said, seemingly appalled.

'Is there a toilet in this restroom?' I replied, confused.

She looked at me as if I'd just got off a plane from Vulgaria, vaguely gesticulating to a distant escalator to remove me from her presence.

Jay then clarified for me that 'toilet' was not a word to be bandied around in polite Manhattan society. Thereafter, I made a point of asking specifically for the toilet whenever possible.

Dinner was yet another meal out. It had become clear that many people in Manhattan didn't use their designer kitchens much, that they were just for show. We met up with an old school friend of Jay's, who took us to a trendy new vegetarian restaurant with phenomenally high prices. His wife twittered about her new 'platform clogs' and all my newly maternal brain could think about was how potentially dangerous they were, if one were wearing them whilst carrying a baby. My worth-its-weight-in-gold, skewered, ostensibly fire-roasted, aubergine was on the raw side, however, and took a lot of chewing, rendering me goat-like. I was, therefore, barely able to take part in the conversation.

What I had ordered was, I thought, similar to one of my own early efforts at cooking with the indomitable Mrs. Shackleton. I envisioned her at the restaurant's kitchen hatch rebuking the chefs, 'Has it truly come to the pass that you have to be told to turn up the grill in order to properly cook an aubergine!' It would have been the sensible thing to have told the waiter that my meal was inadequately cooked but, recalling the woman with the egg, I didn't want to complain. As I chewed away, I noticed one of the kitchen workers had entered the restaurant from the street, bedecked in the checkered trousers and white jacket of a chef. Before walking through the swing doors into the kitchen, he scanned the restaurant, brimming with affluent vegetarians and then, quite pointedly, stuffed his hand down his pants and scratched his crotch a few times. I felt as if I were the only person to notice this as everyone else in the restaurant was busy chattering and posing in their designer fair trade linens. I wondered if he did this each time he arrived for his shift as a sort of 'up yours' gesture that he knew he could get away with as the clientele of the restaurant didn't take any notice of 'little' people.

We didn't realise it yet but our visit thus far had been most unsettling for Jane. We'd only been there three nights but it had apparently been too much for her to cope with. Not only had there been crumbs on the breadboard, but we had left baby booties on the Eames footstool and had not shut the door of the closet properly. Regrettably, it had swung open, unnerving a three-year-old client when our roll of bedding had suddenly emerged, making it akin to a scene from *The Mummy Returns*. When the mummy did return that evening, Jane informed us that she'd made arrangements to billet us at Jay's father's more casual apartment in Brooklyn.

Jay had previously spoken to me about his father, Alvin, describing him as an introverted, small, hirsute man with a 'moss-like beard growing over most of his face' and hiding behind large-lensed trifocal spectacles, beneath which the rampant growth of his wiry eyebrows was held in check, albeit obscuring his vision. In the early 1960s, his father, at that time a grand master of punch-card software, had made the outlandish prediction that computers would soon fit into something far smaller than the average garage, and would even, one day, be carried in a briefcase.

There was a strained atmosphere in the apartment in Brooklyn as we sat around a table eating French patisserie. Dick and Jane, who'd driven us over, had been hesitant to accept the invitation to stay a while. Alvin, his third wife, Dana, and their thirteen-year-old daughter, Anya, tried to engage them in chit-chat but there were plenty of awkward silences.

At one end of the apartment, old newspapers and magazines were stacked in knee-high piles. When he wasn't out on his punishing twelve hour shifts as Chief Systems Analyst of a big bank, Alvin liked to go through these periodicals, which went back ten years, and snip out articles to send to people who were interested in the various topics within them, in a pre-virtual version of the now popular practice of pressing the 'share' button for articles online. Dana confided in Jane, in a moment of current-to-former wifely camaraderie, the intense aggravation of being married to the obsessive com-pulsive Alvin, to which Jane gave a goose-like honk of agreement.

When everyone had finished their triangles of tart, Dick said to Jane, 'Well, are you ready to roll, kiddo?' and they departed. No plan was made as to when they'd next see the grandchild whom they were supposedly on call to adopt at the drop of a hat.

As soon as they were gone, Dana started teasing Jay, calling him 'Mr. Monkey from the Zoo' and addressing me as his 'Maid of the Moment'. It was true, Jay had been prolific when it came to girl-friends in the past, but he was giving every sign that I'd last more than a moment, especially now there was a child on the scene. Then she turned her attention to Alvin and there commenced a sort of smiling sniping between them, which was uncanny in its similarity to the passive-aggressive nastiness of couples in Pinter plays I'd read and performed in, but in a sort of Americanised form. I'd describe it as a battledore of sardonic wisecracks, the subjects of which remained ambiguous to me as I wasn't privy to the details of their unusual relationship. The last time Jay had been in Brooklyn, a couple of years before, things had got so ugly between Alvin and Dana one Sunday that he had removed Anya from the apartment to prevent her being exposed to any more of it. It looked to me as if things were still almost as bad between them now. The sleeping arrangements of the family puzzled me, with all of them reposing in just one of the two small bedrooms, but with Alvin consigned to a single bed by himself in the corner. Dana insisted they sleep under enormous eiderdown quilts with the air conditioning on full pelt in the hot, humid New York summer.

It wasn't long before Alvin took his leave of the connubial sniping, claiming that he had to return to work. We quickly made a plan to go to the Brooklyn Aquarium with Anya but Dana complained about her going out in very short shorts. Anya was defiant and said she wouldn't get changed. On our return journey, we realised we'd accidentally left a day pack we'd borrowed from Dana on the subway. She was so livid with us that we decided to go out again, which was hard with a baby in the sweltering heat.

We came back after dark but Alvin still hadn't returned from work. We tip-toed down the narrow corridor to the spare bedroom and turned on the light, where I recoiled at the sight of a foot-long centipede scuttling off the pillow and disappearing through a crack where the wall met the floor. It happened so quickly that Jay hadn't seen it. When I described what I'd just seen, Jay told me that when Anya was smaller, she was too scared to sleep in her bedroom because of 'the bad caterpillar', as she'd described it, but her parents had never believed her.

Jay had never seen it but had given her the benefit of the doubt, suspecting it might be an escaped tropical 'pet'. We spent the night with the light on, one eye half open and the baby wedged safely between us.

Alvin had already left for work when we got up just after seven the following morning. When we attempted to tell Dana about the centipede, she told us to 'shut up' because we'd give her daughter nightmares. Anya jumped in with 'You see, it's true!' which only annoyed Dana more. As Anya was gathering up her books for school, Dana bawled at us to leave her house which was going a bit far as Alvin paid for everything. She'd given up her secretarial job on marrying him, taking it for granted that, from the age of thirty, she'd never be called upon to work again. Her main occupation now was driving her daughter to and from her private girls' school in Manhattan, where she strove to keep up with the other, much richer, mothers, with whom she'd occasionally meet for lunch, at which times, no doubt, they took it in turns to complain about their meals and send them back to the kitchen. Dana had grown increasingly bitter about not having the money to properly compete with the other mothers, but what she lacked in bills, she sought to make up for in brass.

Just before Dana slammed the door behind her, she reminded us to be gone by the time she returned. Stunned and with nowhere to turn, Jay and I went to the kitchen and tried to eat some breakfast while, at the same time, formulating a plan of where to spend our remaining eleven nights in America. We didn't have the kind of money to cover a stay even in an economy New York hotel and I didn't like the city anyway.

The kitchen where we were sitting was a professional chef's dream, with bright copper pans hanging from the ceiling, a six burner gas cooker with double oven, a set of expensive knives in a butcher's block holder and granite worktops. The trouble was, Dana had barely cooked for over five years; the most she'd do was fry up a chicken burger for Anya, or boil up some pasta onto which she'd toss some gourmet pre-made sauce. She'd become a connoisseur of ordering in, without a care for the cost. Her spendthrift ways helped ensure her husband worked interminably long hours, thereby keeping him out of her house.

'I'd like to go very far away,' I sighed, fed up with how this holiday that I had been reluctant to take with such a small baby, had panned out. 'Can we get on one of those Greyhound buses and just keep going to the end of the line?'

Jay took me at my word. We set off for the Greyhound bus station in midtown Manhattan. While we were waiting for a bus that was going all the way up to Canada, we went to get a frozen yogurt, which was a novelty to me. Before us in the line was a well dressed young man, complaining about what he'd received. 'Not again,' I lamented.

'Look, I distinctly asked you to put the vanilla on top of the chocolate and not the chocolate on top of the vanilla!'

The cowed frozen yogurt vendor, a young Korean woman, was taking his order back and preparing another.

'Why does it matter? Why is the position of the flavours important?' I piped up and everyone in the queue suddenly turned and stared at me as if I might get shot at any moment, which was possible even over a frozen yogurt disagreement. But I was emboldened with indignation, ready to die a martyr in the crusade against fussiness over nothing. I took up the gauntlet again with, 'I mean, really, how could that matter?'

'Mind your own business!' the man sniffed.

But I was on a roll. I'd had enough of the opinionated tribe of the Manhattanites and carried on with, 'It's a power thing, isn't it? You feel you have to lord it over frozen yogurt vendors as those you're obliged to wait on no doubt lord it over you?'

But he didn't answer me, nor would he even look in my direction. It was as if I'd just said the word 'toilet' and disappeared through a hole in the ground.

The journey to Canada included some interesting events, such as when a group of Amish people boarded the bus in far upstate New York. Despite avoiding eye-contact, one of them appeared to be fascinated with the canvas baby carrier I was using and sketched it, no doubt planning to make a prototype on a treadle sewing machine at home. Later, an extended Hasidic Jewish family boarded. They were clearly using the Greyhound bus to move house as a precariously stacked wagon of cases, including dismantled beds and rolled up carpets was somehow all fitted into the cargo hold beneath the bus.

We got out at Wolfe Island on Lake Ontario, where we found a room for a week in a lighthouse which had been converted into a hostel. For the first time since we'd arrived in New York, we were able to relax and recover, spending most of our time lazing on a blanket by the lake. It was refreshing to be away from the tense, class-ridden city. There was no one threatening us with eviction, no pointless arguments and no one fussing about the food they received.

Remembering we had missed a pre-arranged lunch with his aunt, Jay called her from the pay phone at the lighthouse hostel. He related to her our awful shunting from parent to parent, by which she wasn't at all surprised. She was going up to her house in upstate New York, which was on the way back from where we were staying, and asked if we'd like to spend the last part of our trip there with her and her husband. Of course, we jumped at the offer instead of heading back to the City.

Jay's Aunt Grace and Uncle Morty owned a plot the size of a football pitch with a small, deep, clear pond where it was fun to watch crayfish through a snorkeling mask. There were some mosquitos buzzing around the pond and our daughter was nipped. A droplet of blood formed, the first blood I'd ever seen on her, and it gave me a start, a defining moment that made me fully realise how protective I'd become. Grace and Morty's garden was slightly plagued by an animal I'd never seen before, the groundhog, but I thought they were cute and secretly tossed titbits to them, as well as to the numerous little stripey chipmunks, which were also creatures new to me. There was a strong fence around the plot to prevent wolves, bears or uninvited humans entering. In fact, the whole area for miles around was a warren of fenced plots, some of which featured signs reading, 'Trespassers will be shot!', which made trying to take a walk daunting. A drive to the nearby supermarket was about the only local journey one could make without being thwarted.

Morty was proud of his home cinema, which had a library of films on a costly cutting-edge medium that had never really taken off, LP record-sized 'Laser Discs'. To my delight, we watched all the early films of Woody Allen in the evenings. He'd been in the uncle's class at high school, where he'd been, as Morty described him, an 'irritating nebbish' called Allan Konigsberg.

Morty had a huge collection of books about World War II, most of them with 'Hitler' emblazoned on the spine, which must have been the first thing he and his wife saw when they woke up in the morning as they filled a wall of shelves opposite their bed. Jay explained that his uncle had long been obsessed by the thought of the fate that would have befallen him, his wife and their families had their immediate ancestors not made the fortuitous decision to immigrate to the United States at the turn of the twentieth century. Morty, an excellent cook, entertained us at mealtimes with a stock of lengthy jokes to illustrate every human situation. In the long, hot afternoons, he challenged each of us to games of checkers and Chinese checkers and seemed astounded when, once or twice, he didn't win. Jay had suspicions that he'd actually allowed it to happen in order to boost our confidence as he was a man highly experienced in such games, and an elder wizard of Wall Street of inordinate cleverness.

Grace, a psychoanalyst, went out of her way to talk me through my experiences with Jay's unusual parents, while she sat knitting a colourful baby blanket for our daughter, or pieced together a complex jigsaw puzzle which, she maintained, was symbolic of her psychoanalytic cases back in New York. Finally, I had met welcoming and friendly members of Jay's family but it had all happened rather late in our stay. The day soon came to leave the clammy climate of the Catskills and return to chilly, rainy Marsden, the prospect of which I found myself unexpectedly looking forward to.

20

Consorting with one's Betters, a Guide

Earlier that year, in Spring, I had sent off a letter of application in my best handwriting for a teaching position in a small town in comparatively sunny Devon, part-time due to the baby. I only realised when I read the reply on sumptuous bonded paper with a full colour prospectus enclosed, that it was a fee-paying school. I recollected the curious little marching soldiers at the private school opposite my meagre bedsit in York and, with trepidation, rang to confirm the interview.

The following week, accompanied by Jay and our month-old baby, I travelled down to Devon. It was still the days when interview expenses were covered and they even put us up in a quaint old bed and breakfast for a couple of nights. I had never set foot in a private school before and, considering my patchy secondary school education, I was sure this place would never have contacted me had they known the full story. Giving myself, as they might've said, 'a fair crack of the whip', I smiled my way through the interview, trying to be appropriately refined in both speech and actions although, at times, it was a challenge not to reveal how out of my depth I felt.

During my tour of the school I was taken into the staff room, a commodious chamber, lined with oak bookshelves stocked with leather-bound tomes, oil paintings of former headmasters and a grand fireplace. In this room, two elderly 'masters' as they were known, were guffawing and leaping about as they played table football with screwed up wads of paper and flat-bottomed sugar basins on the long polished table in the centre of the room. I'd never seen old men display the bravado of boys like this and I was enthralled. I deduced that what I was seeing were two old fellows who'd gone directly from childhoods spent at boys' boarding schools, onward to Oxford or Cambridge, and then full circle, back to a teaching career in a boys' boarding school, so that they'd never quite grown up. They were 'Old Boys' in the alumni and actual sense.

After my tour, I waited outside the Headmaster's office for my interview. Even in my twenties, I still felt nervous about headmasters, something that went right back to my infant school days. With a shudder, I recalled the very first time a headmaster had spoken to me, in a packed school assembly hall, whilst all of us children sat in neat rows on the hard parquet floor, legs crossed and backs straight. Being in the first year of school, I was in the first row, and the headmaster, Mr. Nailer, was at the front. 'Do you like me?' he'd asked, craning down to the child at the end of my line. He was giving a talk about how we should all like each other. The obedient child answered, 'Yes', but I had heard that naughty children were sent to Mr. Nailer to be caned, so I did not like him. I was afraid of him.

He worked his way down the line, moving closer and closer until finally, he reached me and asked his question. Everyone in the school had their eyes on me, but I could say nothing. 'Well...do you like me?' he coaxed. Still, I could not speak. I stole a glance at the teachers, all women, standing along the sides of the hall. My teacher, Miss Read, was glaring at me but others were suppressing laughter behind their hands and I knew, in that instant, that they didn't like him either. He asked me yet another time before, thank goodness, he gave up and moved on to the next timorous child.

Then there was the time I was sent to Mr. Nailer. The other children watched me do the walk of shame along the corridor to his office. I was certain I would be caned but did not know why. Was it because I hadn't said I liked him in assembly the previous month? I entered the dreaded office and was ushered forward by his nervous secretary. Was she also afraid she was going to be caned? She left me standing in front of his desk, which was clad in fraying laminate and reached almost to my chin. He was sitting behind it, his bald, pink head and his toothbrush moustache looming above, like a face drawn on a balloon. In front of him was the soggy one pound note I had found at morning breaktime, in a pile of autumn leaves near the disused bike shed where I liked to go to mooch around on my own, away from the hullabaloo of all the other children. Was I in trouble because I had strayed from the herd and found a place of quiet meditation amongst rusting bicycles? I'd handed the money in to a dinner lady as soon as I'd found it so surely he didn't think

I'd stolen it?

'This morning, Nyree Forsythe lost her pound note which was her dinner money for this week,' he declared, all the while smoothing and flattening the soggy pound before him on the desk with his fleshy hands. 'Many children would not have handed it in, as you honorably did. They would have kept it.'

As he spoke, I grew increasingly concerned about the soggy pound note. The only thought in my mind was that at any moment it would break in two.

I was jerked from my retrospection by the school secretary of the present, who was not at all nervous and cheerily told me I could 'Go through now'. I stood up, took a deep breath and entered the Headmaster's lair. The man within resembled a giant, ungainly cherub. A lock of his curly hair bounced about his florid forehead as he spoke. Cadbury, his portly chocolate labrador, slumbered peacefully beside his mahogany desk and I began to feel as if I were not going to be caned after all. He went through the anticipated upper class pleasantries of 'I do hope they've been looking after you nicely', and 'Isn't the new turf on the rugger pitch marvellous?' and so on before cutting to the chase. He told me that last week he'd hired three 'top notch' teachers: Titania Ogilvy-Spryte, Tristram Randolph-Wardolf and Charles Hearse, the Third, who were all Oxbridge graduates. I wondered whether the subtext of this was that a school like his couldn't possibly hire someone like me with a degree from an obscure college in the hostile North, and that summoning me for an interview had actually been an oversight. And then there were all these Wodehousian double-barrelled surnames reminding me of Gussie Fink-Nottle, Bertie Wooster's pal, who had a passion for newts, in contrast to my single monosyllabic surname which paled in comparison. Surely, I didn't stand a chance.

At the end of the interview, the headmaster saw me off the premises with 'Cad the Lab', which struck me as an upper class canine parallel to 'Jack the Lad', bringing up the rear. We passed his similarly ungainly ten-year-old son who had just returned from Eton for the holidays. He was struggling with a large wooden coffer which the headmaster told me was his 'tuck box'. Said box was being lugged toward the Headmaster's 'Lodge', a substantial Georgian pile that came with the job.

'That was my tuck box when I was at Eton,' the headmaster fondly reminisced, 'I must say, it gives me a certain pride to see my boy returning with it from its second innings. I do hope he made his tiffin last this time. He's not the finest example of self-restraint, but who can blame him with all the goodies with which his mater furnishes it? We didn't have tiffin like that in my day, I can tell you.'

To my surprise, in light of this tiffin disquisition, I was offered the job a week later. I supposed that there'd been no one else interested as the school was located in an out of the way market town. Being only part-time, I wouldn't really count as a fully-fledged member of staff so they could afford to stick their necks out and give an impression of moving with the times by taking on a non-Oxbridge outsider like me.

So, shortly after returning from New York, Jay, the baby and I moved to Devon by means of the train with two large suitcases and a pram, like a scaled down version of the Hasidic Jewish family on the Greyhound bus in upstate New York. The Head would, no doubt, have been astonished, had he witnessed it. The town we were moving to was of a similar size to Marsden and also had a canal but the crucial difference was that there the water was usually gleaming with sunlight, rather than pitted with rain. On this canal, there was a horse-drawn barge ride that stopped off at a cafe where you could have a cream tea, and where hundreds of teapots on narrow shelves decorated every inch of the walls. There was going to be a lot to look forward to.

We rented a four-storey terrace house with a passion fruit trellis in the garden, from which you could see and hear the plashing convergence of two rivers, a sound which fascinated the baby. Quite soon after we moved in, the baby, with her emergent efforts to crawl, rolled off the couch we were sitting on and our shock at this led to our first ever argument, Jay and I each blaming the other for not watching her properly. Despite our fondness for one another, the baby had become our central focus and would remain so throughout her childhood.

We were lucky in that there happened to be a lot of older people on our street who were fond of babies. Next door to us lived Tom Wall who was spending his retirement restoring antique furniture in the driveway in front of his house. Feeling a bit more settled and slightly richer, we bought a few pieces from him. In the three houses opposite ours, lived kindly upper-crust octogenarians: Anne and Georgie, two sisters who were frequently visited by their brother, a retired elastic band entrepreneur, Ernest an ex-military type with an impressive moustache and marching stride and Meredith who always wore a jeweled brooch on her lapel in the shape of a pair of delicate scissors.

At the end of the street, there was a devout Catholic family with six children squashed into their three-bedroom house. These children were easily identifiable around town as they all looked elfin, like changelings, with blonde hair, almond-shaped blue eyes and pointed features. Appropriately, they had a dozen hutches teeming with pet rabbits at the front. Next door to this family were a retired couple who were active in the Salvation Army and would march down the street in their uniforms. The husband was in the early stages of dementia, however, and could frequently be seen in his front garden rearranging his gnomes. Jay and I speculated that as he grew worse, he was going to start doing the same with the elf children next door.

The town had, as all towns have, its share of unusual characters. 'The Ox', as we referred to him, a giant fellow with tiny eyes and wispy beige sideboards, rolled about the pavements on an adult-sized trike. Another, generally known as 'Rubber Ron', was a septuagenarian who loitered around the marketplace dressed entirely in faux leather and was constantly in the company of ferret-like adolescent boys for whom he regularly bought chips, pies and, so it was said, amphetamine and barbiturate pills.

At the edge of the town centre, Ulrike, a German woman newly arrived in England, had leased a commercial space where, we were pleased to see, she was setting up a vegetarian cafe. As we walked past one day, she asked us to help her improve the English on her menu, so we suggested a few alterations such as changing her 'smooth puree of tomato soup' to 'cream of tomato soup' and her 'appel crumple' to 'apple crumble'. The dilemma was, vegetarianism was not yet popular in the Devonian backwater and when she opened the cafe, we became her main and often her only customers. Possibly part of the problem too was that she was not exactly the healthiest looking advertisement for vegetarianism as she had the aspect of the women from the painting *Dance at Molenbeek* by Pieter Bruegel the Younger: shapeless, pale and with a bewildered expression.

The school in which I was working had been founded over four hundred years ago as a charitable institution for poor boys, but had since descended into being a going concern for anyone who could pay. Exam results, therefore, were mediocre, and it was a rarity for one of the pupils to fulfil the original purpose of an English public school by gaining admission to Oxbridge, despite graduates of those storied halls standing at every blackboard as a sterling example. Nevertheless, there were many old English public school traditions still in place, such as the annual fourteen mile cross-country race, largely over Autumn leaves, and hence known as 'The Rustle', the winner of which received 'school colours' in the form of a garishly striped blazer nipped in at the waist. Colours were doled out mainly for sporting prowess and those who received them generally lorded it over their less sportive peers who wore the plain navy blazer. However, should the wearer of a striped blazer be caught with a can of lager, or breaking some other hallowed rule, they would be stripped of their colours before a committee. Latin Prayer was another custom still going strong. This was held 'in chapel', a faux-Gothic church in the school grounds to and from which 'the masters' would walk 'in procession', their academic gowns, bearing their particular Oxbridge college's colours, flapping in the wind. I was fortunate to have an excuse that got me out of participating in this pomp and circumstance: I, a poor working class girl, had hired my gown at my graduation—ah, the ignominy of it!—and had none to wear.

Due to numbers gradually falling over the years, the school had recently gone co-ed, which was to include staff as well as pupils. I was in the first wave of new female teachers, which coincided with the initial intake of girls. Prior to this, women had only been seen partially obscured behind the curtains of the boarding houses where they lived with their housemaster husbands, or adjacent to the head-master's office, typing up whatever he'd hastily nattered into his Dictaphone. At the first staff meeting just before term began, some of the old masters had flinched at the sight of us new female teachers. It had been decided in advance that we were to be called teachers as 'mistresses' didn't sound quite right. The old masters had been forced to swallow their pride, however, as the customs of a lifetime were going to have to change if the school were to stay afloat.

A biology graduate from Budapest University had

been hired as a lab assistant and to help in the new girls' boarding house as 'second matron' for a year. She had taken the menial job to improve her English. As soon as they saw her, the old chaps in the staff room almost keeled over. Zsa-Zsa was six foot tall with powerful features straight out of a Soviet Realist sculpture. She wore very short skirts from which extended long, tanned and gleaming bare legs. She often sat with me at breaktimes drinking coffee and, not being well-versed in the crossing of one's legs in such attire, used to make the old fellows quite flustered. Trapped on the school campus by endless boarding duties, she was sexually frustrated. One of the younger masters had screwed up the courage to ask her on a date but he was a pasty fellow with a buzzing voice who, even in her sex-starved state, she felt she had to refuse. When she left at the end of the year, I overheard one of the old masters telling another, 'Such a shame Zsa-Zsa has gone; having her here was like being served chocolate cake twice a day.'

During morning break, I would get a much-needed coffee and a couple of biscuits from the trolley and sit down and have a chin wag. A handful of masters, however, regarded breaktime as an opportunity to trot about with lists, asking if so-and-so could be released from being a reserve on the rugger team in favour of keeping the wicket at a forthcoming away game of cricket, and so on. One such fellow, whom some of the masters referred to as 'Thistledown', was the worst for these breaktime scamperings. Bantam-sized, with some floaty down upon his thinning scalp along with a patchy beard, he would approach his fellow masters with a palm-sized memo-pad and a sharp little pencil. His requests were not about sport, but concerned the debating society or play rehearsals. His dialogues invariably went something like this:

'Clive, I've got a clash with your Latin quiz club tomorrow night, and I really must squeeze in another *Timon of Athens* rehearsal. Could you spare Fairfax-Bramble, Chafer-Fortesque and Legge?'

'Egg? Who the hell is Egg?'

'No, Legge, as in Legge, Younger, brother of Hugo from the First Eleven.'

'Yes, you can have 'em this time; don't ask again.'

'Ah, there's one more, just one, mind you. Monty-Spooner.'

'I don't have that boy.'

'Oh yes you do, I have his name on this list from the headmaster's secretary.'

'Monty what?'

'Spooner.'

'Do you mean Montgomery-Spooner?'

'Yes, I just call him Monty to save time.'

'Well, I wouldn't, his father would be livid.'

'Right-ho, point taken, I'll be sure to use his full moniker in future. Can you do without him?'

'What? No, he's one of our adjudicators so you can bugger off.'

'Oh, blast, that'll muck up my rehearsal, are you certain I ca—'

'Yes, I am certain, now be off with you, man!'

A few cultural differences began to emerge between myself and my colleagues that got me into 'a spot of bother'. For instance, the headmaster intercepted me in the corridor one afternoon and asked for 'a quick word', which alarmed me, given my infant school conditioning. The word turned out to be in regard to a cheese and potato pasty which he had observed me eating down the hill in the town centre as he'd driven past in his Bentley. I hadn't realised that the staff code of conduct stated that teachers, like pupils, were forbidden to engage in the unseemly act of eating in the street.

On another 'quick word' occasion, The Head reproved me over the electric pink tights I had worn to school the day before which had, in his opinion, been a little on the bright side. I found this odd in light of his never having said a thing to Zsa-Zsa about her perpetual lack of tights of any hue. Once, he had even found himself compelled to dispense with the 'quick word' method altogether, presenting me instead with a frown that spoke volumes, except that I had no clue as to what it was about. The following day a typed memo from 'The Headmaster's Secretary' appeared in my pigeon hole, in which he enquired rhetorically, 'Surely, you do realise that your paint-splattered clothes last week were unsuitable even for a mufti day?' Apparently, he'd crossed my path without my noticing him as I was leaving the theatre following a session of painting a set for a few hours in my old clothes after the school day.

Being the only other drama teacher in the school, Thistledown quickly decided that I was someone to compete with. When Thistledown directed a play, so he confided to me, he plotted all the actors' blocking on a chess board beforehand and wrote it down in the in the margins of his script. He had a set of standard actor poses up his sleeve, such as head-clutching for characters undergoing frustrating circumstances, or other stock gestures in a similarly melodramatic vein. He did not take it well when, during my first week at the school, the pupils raved about my drama classes with all their exciting warm-up routines and an emphasis on movement rather than lines.

The matter came to a head on the first night that two plays, one directed by each of us, were to be performed. I was to go first with my hour-long production with the younger pupils, for which Thistledown had allocated me the generous budget of one hundred pounds. After the interval, he would follow up with his full three hour version of Two Gentlemen of Verona with the older pupils, for which he had allocated himself a budget of one thousand pounds. He viewed my production as more or less the warm-up to his imminent masterpiece.

I had also decided to do Shakespeare, and had cut *A Midsummer Night's Dream* to its dramatic and comic bare bones. As the money for my show couldn't stretch to any set, it was done on a bare stage with only the flats that I'd painted white, and using lighting effects to highlight ensemble movement. I had visited every charity shop in town, as well as the nearest city, in order to economically deck out my large cast in a suggestive semblance of Edwardian fashion. The characters in the court had high breeches and bustles, while the characters in the forest were more liberated, in what was basically Edwardian underwear: bloomers, petticoats, long johns and the like. The trouble was that the audience of pupils, staff and parents went wild for my show, and not just at the curtain call. There were bursts of applause and uproarious laughter throughout, expressing delight in the skills of the third and fourth formers. At the end of the performance, the headmaster sprang up, forgetting all about cheese and potato pasties and my previous inappropriate attire, to proclaim from the front of the theatre that my work with the pupils had just confirmed unequivocally that the introduction of coeducation at the school had been a resounding success. In the wings, Thistledown clutched his head and tugged his unruly beard, wondering aloud how his bombastic rendition of *Two Gentlemen of Verona* could credibly follow this.

Meanwhile, at Ulrike's vegetarian cafe, things had turned tense. She had been in a relationship with another lady for whom she had immigrated to Devon, but had, without warning, found herself more and more attracted to Freddy, a local fellow who'd briefly been the drummer of a 1980s one-hit-wonder pop group from County Durham. His existence was thereafter blighted by the great bane of the rock and roll lifestyle, ergo he had fallen victim to drug abuse which had left him permanently damaged. Freddy was a gaunt man with a long, drooping moustache and could only walk with the aid of a walking stick. The focus of Ulrike's infatuation, however, was his lank, waist-length brown hair.

Our friend, Dave, was visiting us and we were patronising Ulrike's cafe almost daily. It was coming up to closing time and we were just finishing off our

coffee and cake. As usual, we were the only customers in the place. Suddenly, Ulrike burst through
the swinging kitchen door armed with a bread knife
shouting in her German accent, 'Get out! Get out!'.
Of course, we all just sat and stared, but then it
came again, 'Get out now! I am closing! It is five
o'clock! I have had enough from you always sitting
around in here!' This puzzled us as we were her only
regular paying customers. However, we sensed that
if we didn't remove ourselves forthwith, she'd throw
the crockery at us at the very least.

Later in the week, I happened to hear sobbing as I
walked past the cafe and tiptoed inside with caution.
Ulrike, lay draped across one of the empty tables,
weeping into a paper napkin. I asked her what the
matter was.

'It's Fweddy! He don't want to see me no more!
But I love him! I love his hair!'

'Freddy? That chap with the stick and the tash?'

'Yes! I love his hair and his stash!'

'Really? Even that drooping tash?'

'Yes!'

'Is that why you wanted to get us out last time?
Was he coming to visit you?'

'Yes! He came here evewy day to eat vegetawian
food wit me but he don't want to come any more! We
had welations upstairs all last week and now I love
him! I love his hair so much! He said he don't like to
make welations wit me but I cannot stop thinkin' of
his hair!' And, seemingly in a trance, she ran her
fingers through his imaginary hair before her.

The cafe was temporarily shuttered owing to
Ulrike's overwhelming angst and, very soon, she

could no longer pay the rent. So, after leasing the building for six months, she returned to Baden-Baden to have her nervous breakdown at home with her parents over being deprived of Fweddy and his hair.

As Jay was a happy-go-lucky chap and a dab hand in a kitchen and with no job at that moment, he offered to take over Ulrike's lease, hopeful that he could turn the cafe around. Unfortunately, despite Jay's rising at dawn each morning to begin chopping vegetables for a wide variety of tasty dishes, the cafe barely broke even and was a slog for the three months he tried to make a go of it, with me also coming in before I went to school to help bake cakes, all of this with a baby bumbling around in a play pen. Customer numbers were barely more than in Ulrike's time and often Jay would give the unsold food to hungry students from the local further education college who'd spent their dinner money on cigarettes.

My stint in private school lasted two years and things always remained a little prickly with Thistledown. The new Oxbridge colleagues who'd started at the same time as me were all gone by the time I left. The other female teacher, Titania, decided she hated teenagers and disappeared into the world of academia. Charles had a nervous breakdown and was whisked away in the middle of the night, while Tristram, always overly friendly with one or another of the sixth form girls, was 'asked to leave' and skedaddled off to the South Pacific. What mattered, in the end, however, was that, after a dozen years of uncertainty, I had finally regained proper pride and confidence in myself in the knowledge that I'd performed better than well in my first professional post, whilst remaining a content and caring mother and partner.

21

Valediction in a West Cumberland Churchyard

Manda had been taken to hospital. When her older son, Eric, had not been able to reach her on the telephone, he had gone over to her house to check on her. He found her collapsed outside her bedroom. She was still breathing but she'd had a massive stroke and her old body had dropped to the ground in her nightdress. She had been rushed to hospital but would never regain consciousness. Eric, sitting by her bedside, had heard her speak just once. As if in a dream, she had said 'Eric, put the kettle on'. A few days later, she died.

Meanwhile, my father had been in Yorkshire catching up with old drinking pals, having a holiday away from his launderettes in Thailand. When he heard the news, he'd driven over to visit his mother in hospital. She was the only steadfast feature of his life, never wavering despite his often disagreeable behaviour. When he realised it was likely that she would die, he took the next plane back to Thailand. This behaviour was regarded by family and friends as callous, which it was, but in light of his subsequent inability even to approach Manda's grave, I came to believe that something else lay beneath it. Seeing his mother fading had forced him to face not only her mortality, but also his own. He had been afraid and had run away.

Before going up to the Methodist Church for the funeral, people gathered in Manda's two-up two-down, where there was standing room only. Jay was there with me, fascinated to finally see the house I'd told him so much about, with its furniture all on a miniature scale so it could fit into the little sitting room. I felt overwhelmed by her tiny place being so crowded after all the hours just Manda and I had sat in there.

I walked about with a tray of hot tea in Manda's china beakers. It was January in Whitehaven and it would be freezing in the churchyard. We needed to fortify ourselves. There was some of Manda's home-made shortbread still in one of the biscuit tins in the cupboard under the stairs that I had raided so often and I offered that about too, taking one myself as a last little piece of her.

A distant relative mistook me for my older sister and told me I'd have come in very handy with my 'legal know-how' when his daughter was trying to secure maintenance from her dastardly ex-husband. I smiled and thanked him before moving on. I found it amusing that I'd been muddled up with 'the brainy one', as Manda described my oldest sister to her friends, the first of our clan to go to university. Less than a century earlier, Manda's illiterate grand-parents on the Isle of Man had signed their names in the parish register with an X. She had looked after this sister as a baby and toddler while our parents, barely out of their teens, were cutting their teeth on the world of work. Manda attributed my sister's abundance of brain power to feeding her tins of pilchards while she was in her care. I remember asking Manda one time how she described me to friends and she had said as 'the funny one'.

The church was packed because so many people had known her. Being a larger lady than May, Manda's coffin, courtesy of Mr. Casket at a neighbourly discount, was noticeably wider, longer and in a darker, sturdier-looking wood. Wiff had been buried in the Methodist churchyard, in the vicinity of Manda's parents and siblings. After a twelve year absence, she would be joining him there today, moving from the sagging, little double bed in the back bedroom to the firmer, longer lasting one in the earth.

Unlike May's funeral, the hymns rang out loud and clear because the choir was in attendance. Manda had signed up for church coffee mornings as there were complimentary refreshments for pensioners in return for taking part in a spot of prayer. It now transpired that there was a final perk in the form of the choir singing at the funerals of coffee morning attendees.

During the time when I barely went to school, I had gone to a few services in this very church with Manda for something to do. We never partook of communion but one day I'd tricked her, nudging her to get up, but then not following her down the aisle. She had ambled up to the altar, looking about her, confused, because she'd never taken communion before. I tried not to laugh as she took the wafer in her hand when the vicar had tried to put it directly into her mouth and then, when he offered her a sip of communion wine, she took the goblet from him and drank off a draught. He had gone to get another rather than attempt to wrest it from her. Kneeling, she had looked at the sparse congregation behind her, smiling and nodding at all the people she was acquainted with and trying her best to finish off the bitter wine politely.

My daughter was starting to wriggle in the cramped space, a prelude to tears, so I nipped out before the end of the ceremony. As it was drizzling, I stood rocking her inside the church porch. The coffin suddenly appeared, pushed out of the church on a chrome trolley at breakneck speed in a bid to get it into the grave before the mourners arrived. I had to back into the corner to get out of the way and caught a glimpse of the small brass plaque with *Amanda* engraved upon it. It would have been better if *Manda* had been engraved, as that is how everyone had known her. The man pushing the trolley in such haste had a bald head, apart from long strands of hair at the back hanging over his collar, an archaic look I'd seen on undertakers in old illustrations, or televised adaptations of nineteenth century novels

The church emptied out and we made our way over to the graveside. By the time we got there, the coffin had already been placed in the ground atop a sheet of artificial turf, perhaps the sight of those walls of earth, with their obligatory worms, was considered too grim for the mourners. A group of gravediggers was waiting under an old wrought iron shelter, having a cigarette and sharing some quiet laughter.

A few years later, when my father was no longer working and had moved back to Whitehaven, I asked him to drive me to Manda's grave because I wanted to plant some lavender there. He walked through the churchyard with me, but hung back when his mother's grave came into view. He told me to go on alone and when I looked over my shoulder at him, he was staring at the ground with his hands in his pockets, looking like a little boy somehow, afraid to approach the headstone. It was at that point I realised that his dashing back to Thailand, instead of staying for his mother's inevitable death and subsequent funeral, had originated from his great fear of losing her, the first and forever foremost, of a string of women upon whom he had always remained dependent for his care. It was so different from when his father had died and he had driven up to Whitehaven for the funeral and been able to laugh about his trousers, half-mast on Eric.

I still had problems with being able to shed tears, even then, at what I realised as I stood there, was the saddest moment of my life. My mother was standing on the opposite side of the grave among friends and acquaintances, and my father and sisters were absent. I, alone, was there to represent her younger son's nuclear family, the inevitable fission of which, just as I entered adolescence, had thrown me into Manda's soft embrace. I stood with Jay, holding our daughter, and realised they had eclipsed that old life now, but that at the start of the long transition, when there had been no one else, Manda had held me up until I had begun again to be steady enough to carry myself. In the grave, her name plaque was starting to be obscured by soil, tossed in by the hands of various relatives and close friends, for many of whom she would gradually fade. Yet, to me, she would always be vivid. 'Thank you, Manda,' I said, 'Thank you. You prepared a table for me and anointed my head with oil...and now my china beaker runneth over'.

Acknowledgements
To James Bloom along with Darka, David, Deborah,
Debs, Heather, Madhulika, Paul, Pamela, Rebecca,
Timothy, Tony & Yasmin whose suggestions helped
me to shape *A Young Lady's Miscellany*.

Thanks also to members of Whitehaven Yesteryears
who shared their knowledge of rum butter and
gurning along with other Cumbrian traditions.

Author website www.aurielroe.com

Visit the Facebook page *A Young Lady's Miscellany*

Read more by Auriel Roe and other memoirists on
www.memoirist.org

See our other publications, memoir and literary
fiction www.dogberrybooks.com